MISSING YOU

FINDING HOPE IN HARDSHIP

BY SUZ HOLMES WITH JENNY WHEELER

Published by Terebinth Estate Publishing
ISBN 978-0-473-30900-8
www.suzholmes.com

To obtain permission to excerpt portions of the text, please contact the
author at iamsuzholmes@gmail.com

Front Cover Portrait: Suzanne Holmes with Misha, Bonnie, Jasmine and
Emerald Holmes.
Back Cover: Mark Holmes.
Cover Portrait by Scott McAulay; www.scottmcaulay.com
Cover Design: Josef Estillore.
For details on the Journeys DVDs contact Rob Harley, rob@meltingpot.tv
MXTV Links: mxtv.org/episodes/broadcasters, mxtv.org/MarkLesleyHolmes
mxtv.org/Warrior_Musicianary

COPYRIGHT CREDITS

In Gratitude - From Suz

I AM THRILLED to be able to say thank you. My life has been filled to overflowing with the most amazing family and friends. I have been richly blessed by the many wonderful people God has brought into my life.

First to my family — Mum and Dad, I love you! Thank you for your love and support especially when the girls were young. My brothers – two of the best men I know. How blessed I am to have you in my life. And to their gorgeous wives – Raelene and Katja, thank you for all your support!

David and Val – when God handed out in-laws He gave me the best. What would I have done without you during Mark's long illness and after? You have blown me away with your kindness, support, love and encouragement. Thank you doesn't even come close to adequately expressing my gratitude.

To every single friend, new and old, too many of you to mention personally – you are loved by me and the girls more than you would ever know. Mark loved you too. Each of you is precious and valued. Thank you for your love and friendship.

In particular, I would like to make special mention of: Neil and Rachel Carter, Stephen and Katherine Pether, Steve and Cathy Wedgwood, Clark and Carolyn Nemeth, Holly and John

Taft (née Robertson), Brian and Jenny Lofroth, Martin and Sue Oxley, Heather Major and her late husband Glenn, David and Lisa Walker, Karen Vince, Marilyn Latkin, Jack and Carole Foster, Phillip and Amanda and last but definitely not least Brenton Partridge – THANK YOU! Such precious friends – all of you have been so encouraging and supportive throughout the last fourteen years. I don't know how I would have coped without each and every one of you. I love you all! And Mark loved you so much too!

To Rob Harley – Thank you so much for including our family's story in the Journey's and Life Stories DVD series and in your latest book, The High Voltage Hedgehog. What an honor it is to be a part of what God is doing through your work.

To Tim and Edye Bisagno – Thank you for writing the Foreword and giving such a special view of Mark. Thank you also for all your love and support over all the years despite the distance.

To my dear friend Belinda Partridge – Thank you for believing in this book so much that you took on the social media side of things. Thank you for the endless hours you spend on the computer making sure it is all working, looking great and glorifying God. Thank you for your support, encouragement and love which never wavered and has seen me through my darkest times. Your friendship has spurred me on in my relationship with Jesus and helped me be more like Him.

Jenny Wheeler – When God brought us together little did we know that we would do such a task for His kingdom. You are such a gift from Him. This book would not have happened without you. I can never thank you enough for your generosity, your time, your constant encouragement, your wisdom, your support and the hours upon hours of volunteer work. I thank God on a daily basis that He brought you into my life and that together with Him we are hopefully glorifying Him and making Him known to others.

My girls – Misha, Bonnie, Jasmine and Emerald. What a journey we are on! The four most precious people in my life. Thank you for being you, each of you so unique and so treasured. Thank you for the fun and laughter, for the advice (especially about what not to wear), for the never ending support, encouragement and love.

It has not been an easy road for the four of you. First, years of watching and helping your Dad during his illness and putting up with me as I dealt with looking after Mark and trying to raise you. Then at such young ages watching your Dad die and dealing with the grief of losing a parent.

You are four of the most courageous, brave, kind and generous people I know. You have my utmost admiration as I watch you give life your best shot, each of you determined to make the most of life and use it to help others – what an inspiration you are! Your Dad was so proud of you all. I am so proud of you all! I love you to infinity and beyond and always will!

Finally – to my Saviour and Lord, Jesus! What do I say to the Creator of the Universe, the saviour of my soul, and the healer of my heart. Thank you for it all! Thank you for not leaving me, but rather for walking with me, carrying me when I needed it and for everything else. Thank you for spurring me on into a life filled with abundance.

Thank you for not letting me wallow in self-pity, but for using your word and your people to encourage and keep me going. Thank you for being miraculous at the perfect times. Thank you that I have a future filled with hope in this life and then an eternity to look forward to in your presence. You have my life and you always will. I love you Jesus!

FOREWORD
TIM BISAGNO, MXTV

MARK LESLIE HOLMES. I just love the sound of that name. I always did. I still do. Filled with the Spirit from the bottom of his black hightop Converse, to the top of his big black dreaded head — I love him. I miss him.

Of all the people I know, I've never met a more immovably stubborn man. Immovable, in his calling. Immovable, in his love for his wife and kids. But 'movable' doesn't begin to describe Mark's heart for those who didn't know Christ. For that, Mark would move a mountain.

Mark was a musician. A good one. Gentle is what he was. But to me and many others, the iconic musicianary is who he will always be. Mark was soft spoken. But 'gentle and soft' are the last two words anyone would ever use to describe the best noise to ever come out of a guitar amp since the creation of distortion. That's when you heard Mark's soul. And what a soul it was. That's when Mark went to battle. Fighting for those he loved: God, and those who did not know Christ.

Distortion may have been his trademark sound, but what will ring much longer than his amp is his very undistorted commitment to the Gospel. Too briefly gracing a world marked with watered-down Gospel theology and a 'more is better' philosophy,

Mark Leslie Holmes had an endearingly simple and contagious love not only for good food, good music and good friends, but also for the simple Good News of the Gospel. That is what will ring the loudest in my heart about Mark, the warrior friend of mine.

Much like David, the warrior-musician from Paul's words in Acts 13:36, 'David served God's purpose in his own generation.' I believe we can all take note of Mark's life as a servant. A servant who was happiest when he was serving — serving God's purpose in his own generation.

Mark Leslie Holmes loved Jesus. He loved Jesus, very much. To this day, Mark's infectious love for Jesus and affecting culture continues to permeate the ministry he partnered with me to begin over two decades ago. Mark blessed me. Mark affected me. Mark blessed his world. Mark affected his culture. It may have been said about others, but it's never been more true — Mark Leslie Holmes left this world and all who knew him better than he found them. By knowing Mark, I am a better man and a better minister of the Gospel of Jesus Christ to this generation.

Upon reading this story of beauty, tragedy, redemption, and more redemption, I pray you too will aspire more greatly, to hear the Good News from The Master as I know Mark did; 'Well done my good and faithful servant.'

TIM BISAGNO | MXTV, rePRESENTING GOD'S WORD
EMAIL: tim@mxtv.org
TEXT: 615.456.1901, WEB: www.mxtv.org
TWITTER: mxtv, FACEBOOK: missionxtv

FOREWORD
TIM BISAGNO, MXTV

MARK LESLIE HOLMES. I just love the sound of that name. I always did. I still do. Filled with the Spirit from the bottom of his black hightop Converse, to the top of his big black dreaded head — I love him. I miss him.

Of all the people I know, I've never met a more immovably stubborn man. Immovable, in his calling. Immovable, in his love for his wife and kids. But 'movable' doesn't begin to describe Mark's heart for those who didn't know Christ. For that, Mark would move a mountain.

Mark was a musician. A good one. Gentle is what he was. But to me and many others, the iconic musicianary is who he will always be. Mark was soft spoken. But 'gentle and soft' are the last two words anyone would ever use to describe the best noise to ever come out of a guitar amp since the creation of distortion. That's when you heard Mark's soul. And what a soul it was. That's when Mark went to battle. Fighting for those he loved: God, and those who did not know Christ.

Distortion may have been his trademark sound, but what will ring much longer than his amp is his very undistorted commitment to the Gospel. Too briefly gracing a world marked with watered-down Gospel theology and a 'more is better' philosophy,

Mark Leslie Holmes had an endearingly simple and contagious love not only for good food, good music and good friends, but also for the simple Good News of the Gospel. That is what will ring the loudest in my heart about Mark, the warrior friend of mine.

Much like David, the warrior-musician from Paul's words in Acts 13:36, 'David served God's purpose in his own generation.' I believe we can all take note of Mark's life as a servant. A servant who was happiest when he was serving — serving God's purpose in his own generation.

Mark Leslie Holmes loved Jesus. He loved Jesus, very much. To this day, Mark's infectious love for Jesus and affecting culture continues to permeate the ministry he partnered with me to begin over two decades ago. Mark blessed me. Mark affected me. Mark blessed his world. Mark affected his culture. It may have been said about others, but it's never been more true — Mark Leslie Holmes left this world and all who knew him better than he found them. By knowing Mark, I am a better man and a better minister of the Gospel of Jesus Christ to this generation.

Upon reading this story of beauty, tragedy, redemption, and more redemption, I pray you too will aspire more greatly, to hear the Good News from The Master as I know Mark did; 'Well done my good and faithful servant.'

TIM BISAGNO | MXTV, rePRESENTING GOD'S WORD
EMAIL: tim@mxtv.org
TEXT: 615.456.1901, WEB: www.mxtv.org
TWITTER: mxtv, FACEBOOK: missionxtv

CONTENTS

INTRODUCTION

'Well, there were three of us in this marriage, so it was a bit crowded.' - Diana, Princess of Wales, in a BBC Panorama interview with Martin Bashir, 1995.

WHEN I MARRIED Mark Holmes on the 9th December 1989, there were 'three of us' in our marriage too, but for us this was its most positive unassailable foundation. I cannot remember a time when I was not passionate about the Lord. Long before I got married, I started every day alone with God, reading the Bible and praying. I would sometimes just sit and listen for the 'still small voice' (1 Kings 19:12) to speak, or wait for the Holy Spirit to lead me to a scripture He wanted to bring to my attention.

Nothing deflects me from this pattern of starting my day with coffee and the Bible. If I have to take someone to the airport to catch a plane at 4:00 a.m., I set my alarm for 2:00 a.m. so I do not miss this 'appointment with God.' It is entrenched in me, so much so that not one day starts without this reflective time. When Mark was diagnosed with brain cancer ten years into our marvellously happy marriage, I decided I would keep a journal. It would serve as a positive way for me to process what I was walking through with Mark's illness and with God.

Feelings that I was unable to speak to others because they might have been shocked by my honesty, I could write to God. Being completely honest with myself and the Lord became a way to cope with the truth of what I was feeling and thinking. I hope what you read here won't shock you. All I can say is it's an open reflection of the turmoil we endured as we wrestled with illness and all the unwelcome things that come through the door with it.

My prayer is that this account may help others to 'bear the unbearable.' This is our story.

PART I-
DOES GOD HEAL?

Where Suz And Mark Ask the Question:
What Do You Do When Jehovah Rapha (the God Who Heals)*
Doesn't Seem To Answer Your Prayers As Expected?
(Exodus 15: 22–26)* 2000 – 2007

CHAPTER ONE
NOT AN AVERAGE LIFE

'My home is in Heaven. I'm just traveling through this world.' - Billy Graham.

GOOGLE THE DATE April 19 and you'll find it is famous for all sorts of reasons, including the day the Protestant church officially began (1529), and the day of the 1995 Oklahoma bombing which killed 168 people. I recall that April day vividly, because my husband Mark and I, with our daughters Misha (nineteen months) and Bonnie (four months), were passing through LAX on our way to begin a new chapter in our lives as edgy young Christian muso-missionaries in Houston, TX.

As the TV screens at Los Angeles International flickered with shocking images of smoking and wrecked buildings, of windows shattered and cars burned out in this domestic terrorist attack, we passed through immigration onto a flight bound for a new job affiliated with the First Baptist Church in Houston. Under the direction of Youth With A Mission (YWAM), we were joining Tim Bisagno to work on Mission X, a start-up venture using music and video to reach Generation X with the gospel.

I had no premonition that five years later to the day, my talented off-beat lead guitarist husband would be lying anaesthetised in an operating theater, undergoing surgery for a possibly malignant brain tumor. Or that on another April 19 day not much later, we'd be sitting in another hospital clinic receiving yet another devastating medical report that would rock our faith to its foundation. Yes, there are certain dates I remember very well, and April 19th is one of them.

The years preceding that appointment in a hospital operating theater had been remarkably happy and fruitful. When we moved to Houston, we'd already spent three years touring Europe and New Zealand with Tim and others on a band schedule that combined alternative heavy rock and talking about Jesus to Punks in Dusseldorf, to ash-tray throwing Berlin night clubbers, to stoned anarchists in Copenhagen's hippy enclave of Christiania and to recently 'liberated' Warsaw Communists.

Based in Amsterdam with YWAM, we were passionate about our music and our faith, traveling in a derelict red van, towing a trailer with a stage coffin on it — part of our props — all over Europe. In their band, The Friendlys, Mark and Tim worked very well together. Mark was lead guitarist who also wrote a lot of the music and sang; Tim was lead singer and also wrote lyrics. When we weren't touring with bands in Europe and the US, we'd been back home in New Zealand, keeping in touch with our supporter base and organizing band tours Down Under.

Mark and I had grown into a tightly bonded unit, producing four beautiful daughters and sharing a deepening love, which fulfilled all our hopes for a loving marriage and joyous family life. So I know with certainty that when we first learned that the crippling headaches Mark had been experiencing were not just due to his 'needing glasses' or 'his neck being out' as doctors and friends had suggested, but were due to a tumor, our reaction to the news was very deliberate. We agreed, 'God is in control and we are not worrying about it.' Until we knew any differently, we would treat it as a benign tumor.

After those years of babies sleeping at my feet in the 'out of bounds' band access area at the back of some stage, we'd ridden the tide of God's purposes for us back home to New Zealand. We'd beached in familiar territory, close to our loved ones. We were both thirty years old, and shared a conviction we needed to give our four girls, aged between one and six, stability and security after a season of turbulence. We had no idea we were about to embark on the most challenging journey we'd ever undertaken together, one that would come close to tearing us apart.

Worrying Symptoms

Just before our tenth wedding anniversary, Mark had started complaining about his vision diminishing. He was also regularly suffering bad headaches. The obvious suggestion was he needed glasses, so off he went to an optician. Sure enough, he was told his eyesight was deteriorating slightly so he got glasses, but the headaches continued to bother him. When his eye problems became so severe that he'd temporarily lose sight in one eye, or he'd have to hold his hand over his right eye when driving because he was seeing double, even Mark, who'd also become unusually grumpy trying to just 'brave it out,' had to concede he needed to see a doctor.

Six weeks after the first diagnosis, we discovered Mark's tumor was not benign, but malignant. Despite this, we still addressed the future with a steady, faith-based confidence. To us it seemed simple: either God would heal Mark, or he would die and go home to be with Jesus. We didn't rush into a flurry of desperate prayer for miracle healing, although friends and fellow church members did come and pray with us. We may have been a little wary of going overboard praying for Mark's healing because of an earlier experience we'd had with seeking healing through prayer.

A young man in the church we were attending was diagnosed with cancer, and the whole church prayed for his healing. When it did not happen and he died anyway, some people became disillusioned with God and dropped away from church altogether. We didn't want the same thing to happen again, so we didn't aggressively chase after prayer for healing, but accepted when it was offered.

Clouds Loom

But we are getting ahead of ourselves . . . The first real indication that Mark's eye problems might have a sinister underlying cause came on a Sunday night early in April 2000 when he was playing guitar at church. He suddenly paused and just stood staring into space with a blank expression. He seemed to be having some sort of lapse in consciousness. Rachel Carter, a very dear friend and the wife of Neil, one of Mark's closest friends and a former band member, was standing near the stage and noticed what was happening. When he regained consciousness, she insisted he go see the doctor the next day. He took her advice.

Mark was on night shift at his video editing job at Flying Start Pictures, so he was at work the next evening when, to my surprise, the doctor Mark had seen that day phoned. Dr. Round quizzed me if I had noticed anything different about Mark's behavior. I mentioned he had been unusually grumpy lately, but I was putting that down to the fact he was working long hours. Dr. Round finished the phone call with, 'If you haven't heard from Auckland Hospital by Wednesday please ring me.' I truly thought nothing of it and when Mark got a call from the Neurology Department of Auckland Hospital on Wednesday for an appointment on Thursday, it didn't enter my head to go with him. I just assumed it was all going to be fine.

Thursday afternoon, Mark rang from work to say that the neurology specialist had made an appointment for him to have an MRI scan the next morning at 7:00 a.m. I was at the girls' ballet class at the time, and I moaned about what a stupid time of day that was for someone with a family to have to get to hospital. Jenny Lofroth (a close friend from church) was sitting with me when I got Mark's call, and she told me I should go with him. I said, 'No way, he'll be fine.'

Mark and I were so sure we had nothing to worry about, but God had given us great friends who thought differently. They organized for Neil to go with Mark to his appointment and Jenny to take me to the hospital to be with him as soon as I got Misha (age six) and Bonnie (five) off to school. Another precious friend, Belinda Partridge, was recruited to babysit Jasmine (three) and Emerald (one). I just didn't see why everyone was making such a fuss.

Completely against my will, as I was sure Mark was just fine, I sat in early morning rush hour traffic and walked into the MRI department just as he was coming out of the scanning session. The radiologist was insistent; we would be given the results later that day and we had to remain in the hospital for the consultation. I really didn't appreciate 'wasting' four hours in a hospital when there was so much to do at home, but Mark was joking and relaxed as we were called into a consulting room so tiny I was sure someone had accidentally made the broom closet into an office. A lovely young doctor began talking, but preoccupied as I was by the household chores awaiting me at home, I had difficulty focusing on what he was saying.

He leaned forward and held up three fingers, as he explained that any one of three things could be responsible for Mark's symptoms . . . A migraine, some kind of tension problem with a long name I didn't recognize, or a tumor. Long silence.

'Unfortunately I am sorry to tell you that Mark has quite a big growth in his brain.'

I stared at him, stunned. Had he just said my husband had a brain tumor? He pulled out some big MRI scans and pointed to a gray egg-shaped circle in Mark's brain. It was massive; it seemed to be taking up the whole front part of his brain. Mark pointed to a tiny dark spot on the scan and asked if that was it. "Is that the tumor?" he asked.

'No,' the doctor replied, 'it's this gray circle here.' Another silence. Mark has a massive brain tumor? Totally inappropriately I quipped, 'Hey, at least we now have proof that you actually have a brain, Mark.'

We laughed, because we felt there wasn't much else we could do. The doctor continued, 'Because of the size of it, we will need to organize surgery as soon as possible. You will be hearing from Neurosurgery within the week. Mark, you are not allowed to drive anymore or go to work.

'It is most likely a benign tumor, so nothing too much to worry about, but of course we will have to get a biopsy, and because that involves brain surgery, the surgeons will go in and take as much of the mass out as they can. Again I am very sorry.' With those words we were walking out of the broom closet.

We looked at each other and asked, 'Did that just happen?' We were in a state of complete disbelief. This had to be some weird dream. I had tears streaming down my face. Mark, with his normal chilled attitude announced he was hungry and suggested we go and find food. So off we went to a McDonald's.

As we sat there, Mark was eating like nothing had happened; I was crying, but not because of the tumor. That was an unknown. I had no immediate feelings about it because I didn't know how to confront a tumor. I'd never had to deal with one before. But I had had plenty of experience of budgeting to feed my family, and in my shock, I seemed to revert to a primitive insecurity.

It was something like; 'I don't know how to worry about tumors, but I do know how to worry about money.' And so I was crying and asking, 'What are we going to do about money?' Even though Mark was working more than full-time hours, he was a freelancer, so wasn't entitled to sick pay or benefits. With this diagnosis, we were instantly deprived of any income.

We realized there were a few people we had to contact immediately; Mark's employers and parents. That second call was hard for Mark to make, and just after we arrived home, his parents arrived at our house. On the drive home, we'd decided we'd do everything within our power to explain to the girls what was happening in a context they could understand.

Strange Premonition

Lying in bed that night, we allowed our thoughts to drift to a worst case scenario. 'What if this is cancer? What if this is terminal?' I remember both of us deciding there and then we were not going to jump ahead of ourselves and worry over what we didn't know. At that moment it was a routine, round, supposedly benign tumor and that was the extent of our knowledge.

God says very clearly in Matthew 6:32–34, 'Don't worry about tomorrow.' So that was exactly what we were going to do. What I couldn't tell Mark was that as we'd stepped out of the hospital I had a distinct impression — the still small voice of the Holy Spirit — telling me 'This will take his life.'

The next day we decided to delay telling anyone else until we knew more. Our church was having a big family camp the next weekend and we didn't want Mark's tumor to be the center of attention. It was also nice to pretend for a while that this really wasn't happening. However, a new drama soon shattered this nice little fantasy.

Our follow-up consultation with the neurosurgeon had been made on a Friday, the day the camp was starting. The doctor looked at the scan, ran off muttering something about the tumor being seven centimeters in diameter and this being urgent, and then came rushing back in with a date for surgery, which was only five days away.

We were shocked they were going to operate so quickly, but consoled ourselves that at least it was after the camp. We could get through that with everyone focused on God. Then the neurosurgeon asked us if Mark had ever had any seizures. We didn't realize that the episodes when Mark went on 'pause' — and there had been more of them since the incident when he'd been playing on stage — were actually petite mal seizures, so we replied in the negative. He told us to be aware they could happen.

On our way home, Mark had his first grand mal seizure. We had called to see our accountant, who worked out of a suburban home office. We had just knocked on his front door when Mark slumped against the door jamb, his body twitching, his eyes half closed. The accountant opened up to find me holding Mark upright and saying something like, 'Mark has just been diagnosed with a brain tumor, and I think he is having a seizure.'

I had no idea what to do, but our amazing God took over. Neil had called Mark's cell phone at the exact same time the seizure began. I told him what was happening, and he rang our doctor, who rang the neurosurgeon, who then rang us, to say Mark was to head back to the hospital immediately. For the next five days Mark was confined to a hospital bed, immobilized by recurrent, potentially brain-damaging seizures from a supposedly benign tumor.

CHAPTER TWO
THE ROAD GETS DARKER

'If there is anywhere on earth a lover of God who is always kept safe, I know nothing of it, for it was not shown to me.
'But this was shown: that in falling and rising again we are always kept in that same precious love.' - Julian of Norwich.

MARK'S SURGERY was scheduled for April 19, 2000 at 8:00 a.m. As far as days go, this was one of the worst. At 7:00 a.m. Mark rang me; we were both scared, having been warned of the many dangers of brain surgery. The perils included the possibility of a stroke, of a part of the brain being permanently damaged, and of death. I tried my best to be positive and to reassure Mark that it would be fine, trying to convince myself in the process. We knew without doubt God was in control, but we also knew that wasn't an insurance policy against death. We ended the phone call in tears.

I busied myself with getting the girls ready for the day. I was taking them to a friend's place to hang out. Neil had become the designated chauffeur for the next six days, and so he took us to her house. We hung out, had coffee and made small talk, but it was hardly a substantial distraction and when I could no longer bear it, I asked to go to the hospital. Mark's surgery was going to be about four hours, and I wanted to be there when he came back to the ward. Nearly two hours passed before the elevator door opened and Mark was wheeled out with tubes sticking out of his head. He looked absolutely dreadful, and I cried as he was wheeled past.

I felt so helpless and scared for him and overwhelmed at how my apparently well husband of just days before was now lying in a hospital bed looking extremely ill. Mark had come out of surgery fine, but then he had a wracking seizure that had left the right side of his body completely useless. The doctors had warned us that brain surgery had its dangers, and they could never predict how someone would come through such a hugely invasive undertaking. Following the seizure, the doctors had done an emergency CT scan looking for potential internal bleeding or signs of a stroke.

A surgeon took me aside with Neil and told me the tumor was definitely cancer, but we would have to wait for the full biopsy results to know how serious it was. The doctor said they had successfully removed 90% of the malignant tissue, but unfortunately couldn't remove it all; the remaining growth was entwined like tentacles into the brain. There were too many risks to remove it. Cancer seemed like the loudest word in the room, magnified in capital letters and booming through a megaphone.

The next six days were horrible. Mark had constant, extremely painful seizures. The doctors pumped him full of morphine and anti-seizure drugs to sedate him. Every seizure did more damage to Mark's brain and had the potential to kill or disable him further. They needed to be stopped, so his brain could recover.

I would leave the house at 9:30 a.m. and return twelve hours later feeling exhausted and completely useless while Mark lay in terrible pain. My daughters were well taken care of by family and friends and our wonderful church provided meals and housecleaning. I didn't have to think about any of this, which was great because I couldn't anyway.

On the sixth day, Mark was finally moved out of neurosurgical intensive care into a normal ward, the seizures under control at last. The hospital considered he no longer needed constant monitoring, but he was still unable to do most things by himself including feeding, walking, and toileting. I left that evening with my normal chauffeur, Neil. As we made our way home, he started to chatter distracting me from thinking about Mark, but this night I was overwhelmed.

We drove in complete silence as I looked out the window with tears streaming down my face. I was unable to stop them and unable to speak. It had been an unspeakably horrible two and a half weeks. My whole body felt as if in heartache. My lovely world had turned upside down.

I had gone from an idyllic marriage and home life, to facing a tumor, then cancer and then watching the man I loved most in the world cope with surgery, seizures and intense pain. I had barely seen my girls, and I had no idea what our future held. In two and a half weeks, my life had become one big mess that I couldn't tidy up. We followed the normal route home, and as we were about to pass my brother's house I yelled, 'Go there'. Before Neil had stopped the car I ran to the door, banged on it until it opened and then fell into my brother, Robert's arms, sobbing.

I had no idea how long we stood there. I think Rob thought Mark had died, but I could not be strong one minute longer and needed someone who loved me unconditionally. My brother was right there. We spent some time with him and his girlfriend Michelle, trying to process the events of recent weeks. Mark was such a loved brother-in-law. He had been part of my two brothers' lives since their early teens, and they accepted him as closest family without reservation. We were all trying to come to terms with what had been thrown at us.

Another Bombshell

As Mark's post-surgery rehabilitation progressed, he had to learn to walk again for the third time in his life. (The second time had been a few years into our marriage when he had suffered a very serious bout of Guillain–Barré syndrome.) His weak condition related not just to the brain surgery, but to the damage caused to his right side by the seizures.

Six weeks after surgery we were seated in another small room, facing another cancer specialist and absorbing more horrible news. The oncologist explained Mark had an anaplastic astrocytoma. In plain English, a Grade 3 malignant tumor (Grade 4 being the worst). It was terminal with or without treatment, but successful treatment would give him a few extra years. In black and white terms Mark had eighteen months to two years to live if the normal course of treatment – six and a half weeks of radiation and six months of chemotherapy — wasn't successful in shrinking the 10% of the tumor that was left after surgery. If the treatment was successful, he had five to seven years. I believe this is referred to as a 'Bombshell!'

As I walked out of that appointment and into the corridor I heard 'three years' loudly and clearly — so audible, it felt like a person was walking beside me and spoke into my ear. We drove out of the hospital about a kilometer, pulled into a car park and cried. We now felt justified in being really upset.

From the first day, we had made the decision not to worry and tried to hold fast to it. Every time we were given bad news, which I might add was every time we saw a doctor, it was never the final bad news. We felt like this was the final blow. We just sat in the car in shocked disbelief and sobbed together. Physical pain seems to accompany deep sadness and that day our hearts felt broken beyond repair.

From then on, we were on a journey that really seemed to take a life of its own – the opposite of our first ten years together. We felt as if we had no part in the decisions taken, no say in what happened or what was done to Mark. Over the next six months, Mark endured radiation and chemotherapy. He experienced claustrophobia as they covered his face with clay for the radiation head mask, and he was violently ill with the chemotherapy, but through it all he maintained a phenomenal attitude.

Nothing ever seemed to faze him, and he took it all in his stride. He didn't work during most of the treatment time. He battled tiredness constantly and small seizures were a normal part of our day. But he thoroughly enjoyed being home with me and the girls. When he was able, he helped with everything and sometimes it just felt like he was on an extended holiday. But it really was no holiday.

By January 2001, the first round of treatment options had been exhausted, and we were faced with another heartbreaking choice. An MRI scan done just before the chemo started and another after the first three treatments of chemo showed the remaining tumor had not shrunk at all.

The oncologist asked us to take some time to decide. Did we want to carry on with the treatment, opting for quantity over quality of life? Or did we want to stop treatment and opt for better quality for the remaining time? We chose quality over quantity. Mark was sent home with eighteen to twenty-four months to live.

I felt sick for days afterward. Coffee and chocolate are my comfort foods and that was all I was able to swallow. I was in utter disbelief. I felt numb one minute and in shocked incredulity the next . . . it was hard to grasp that this was my life, and it was happening to my husband. Then I got pneumonia. I had never had it before in my life, and it was the last thing we needed. My body was probably reacting to my see-sawing emotions. In hindsight, I had to admit coffee and chocolate were never recommended as health foods.

While I was having trouble coming to terms with Mark's prognosis, he was relieved. He wanted to just get on with what life he had left. He hated the tiredness, the frequent trips into Auckland Hospital, which even on good traffic days took thirty minutes and often a lot longer. The treatments had become a drag. He was glad he had time to enjoy being a Dad. He loved his girls so much and was now able to help them with their homework, go to school events and play with them.

CHAPTER THREE
WHEN HOPE HAS GONE

'We're not doubting that God will do the best for us;
we're wondering how painful the best will turn out to be.' -
C. S. Lewis.

FROM FEBRUARY 2001, we set about trying to live what life
we had left with Mark to the fullest. It was a good decision not
to do any more chemotherapy. Mark was trying to enjoy life and
making the most of his time with the girls and me. There were
three things he wanted to do before he died.

The first was getting some tattoos, which he went ahead and
did immediately. The second was to do a bungy jump, which
was vetoed by the medical team because of his brain tumor and
the possible repercussions, but the third — to go sky diving —
was made possible thanks to a group of our friends who got
together and arranged for Mark to go on a tandem skydive.

Mark and one of his closest friends, Matthew Mark, jumped
together. A huge group of family and friends went to watch.
Fun days like this made the reality of the death sentence feel far
away. We had taken lots of family photos and photos of Mark
with each of the girls. They are so precious. Who knew how

long we had left with Mark, and I wanted the girls to have some reminders of his love for them.

But it was tragic trying to live life as fully as possible with a death sentence hanging over us. In particular, I was tired of our finances being a constant struggle. I shouldn't have complained when we lived in a country with a social welfare system that enabled me to stay home and look after Mark and the girls, but what we received on the Invalid's Benefit was not quite enough to pay all the bills, as well as buy food and petrol. There were always more needs than there was money.

We were trying to look to God for strength as we stepped blindly into each day. I knew that God knew what each day would bring and walked before us. Each day we woke up, we never really knew what we were going to have to deal with. My constant prayer was for strength.

Mark and I also really wanted to glorify God through this illness. We wanted people to look at us and see how we were dealing with the illness, the finances, the fact that it was terminal and we wanted them to ask, 'how are they coping so well?' Or 'how do they still have joy?' If we could show one person Jesus through this, it would be worth it.

As the days passed, Mark was experiencing more side effects of the tumor. Some days he suffered from sharp head pains; his balance was wobbly and he often had small seizures. This scared me because I realized Mark was only going to get worse. How was I going to cope? How would I endure watching the man I loved get sicker? How was I going to deal with him dying? There were so many unknowns. I learned to lean heavily on God for guidance and protection, and I found constant encouragement from my Bible.

One particular scripture came to mean a lot to me. Second Corinthians 5:6–9 notes, 'Therefore we are always confident and know that as long as we are at home in the body we are away from the Lord. We live by faith, not by sight. We are confident, I say, and would prefer to be away from the body and at home with the Lord. So we make it our goal to please him, whether we are at home in the body or away from it' (NIV).

I loved the bit that said 'we are away from the Lord.' It's as though we should so yearn to be with Him that we constantly feel away from Him. But I am embarrassed to say that a lot of Christians didn't cope well with Mark's cancer. We had some crazy suggestions from well-meaning people, including the hoary old idea that Mark must have sinned and the cancer was his punishment. The Bible clearly states our sins are forgiven when we ask God for forgiveness and accept that Jesus, (God's son) died on the cross and He took all our sins on Himself. As a result we can freely come before God and ask His forgiveness (Acts 2:38 and Romans 10:9).

Another holier-than-though proposal was that our faith was lacking — that Mark and I didn't have enough faith for Mark to be healed. The Bible says if we have faith as small as a mustard seed (which is the tiniest of seeds) we can say to this mountain to move and it will (Matthew 17:20). I am pretty sure Mark and I had that small amount of faith.

Then there were the people who asked if they could come around and pray for us. Mark and I were like, 'sure, that will be fine.' But the 'prayer session' often turned into an encounter that felt like a verbal attack on how we were doing life — all disguised in sanctimonious prayer. It was devastating and extremely disturbing and also — to be frank — bloody rude.

Our only comfort was that this was not from God – it was from people with their own agendas. God is good and He clearly speaks to us lovingly as His children. But one thing it did was make us wonder what kind of impression we were giving people. We were humbled to think we may not have been giving a good impression. In which case we were failing in our one and only goal — to give God all the glory.

Outliving Predictions

The year 2002 arrived. We had been suffering through for two years. Our goal was to show Jesus to those around us through this illness. I was unsure if we were successful in doing so as we were still trying to cope with just living through what the illness brought each day. I was surprised by the complete loneliness I sometimes felt. But the Lord was always so near, and I found such strength in reading His word. Jesus went through the ultimate loneliness on the cross when He said, 'My God, my God, why have you forsaken me?' (Matthew 27:46, NIV).

I was never going to face that degree of abandonment, but I did feel extremely isolated by Mark's illness. Mark was going down one path with the cancer, and I was going down another path and for the first time in our marriage our paths were not the same. It was terribly lonely and it was something I had never experienced before.

I was always so tired; I seemed to drag myself through the days. I felt like I was the constant slave to five other people. I knew that the girls were just young kids, but the constant arguing, disobedience and the work maintaining family life was exhausting. There were so many times when I just stopped and sat and said, 'I can't take or cope with this anymore' and yet fifteen minutes later I had to get up and somehow find the energy to do what had to be done. I realized that the person who would suffer the most if I didn't keep going was me.

At the end of September 2002, Mark's colleague and friend Lisa Walker rang and told us TV3 (one of New Zealand's nationwide TV channels) wanted to do a documentary on us. We had already been filmed for the *Journeys* series, a shorter video series produced and directed by Rob Harley. Rob told us that he had received a lot of good feedback on our story from churches worldwide that were showing the series, and this sparked an interest from Lisa to interview us in more depth.

We were all very excited as it would be an amazing opportunity to show how Jesus was helping us through this journey of cancer towards death. Because this was a journey towards death, right? That is what the doctors told us, wasn't it?

But as the months turned into years and Mark outlived all his doctors' predictions, it seemed as if in those early years we'd been engaged in some sort of Phony War. Like for the Churchill-led Allies in September 1939, war had been declared but commencement of the real battle was delayed. We'd dawdled in what Sir Winston had dubbed the Twilight War, while full-on engagement was still looming in the future. Looking back, we just had no idea.

A Fifth Child

Mark's sense of enjoyment at being home with the girls gradually leaked away. The almost guilty feeling of 'playing hooky from school' and the determination to make the most of the time he had left also dissipated. Some days he would just cry, because he wanted this journey to be over. But much of the time, he seemed to accept his fate almost too readily. His father David and I often commented that we thought he would have fought harder to preserve his normal activities. He had always been a very easygoing personality, but he had never been lazy. Now he seemed to quite rapidly accept a state of helplessness. He became increasingly self-centered and even infantile.

It made me furious at times, but I had no idea what was going on in his head, or how brain damage might be affecting him in subtle ways. At meal times he behaved like a contrary five-year-old at a birthday party. Often he would want a coffee, so I would make him one. Then he would see one of the girls with a glass of Coke and he would want that too; then someone else would ask for a hot chocolate and he would want that too, and before I knew it, he would have three different drinks as well as his glass of water sitting around him. It was like he was worried he was missing out.

He started sulking if he didn't get what he wanted and asked repeatedly for things until he got what he wanted. This was nothing like Mark's normal behavior before he got ill, and I suspected it was due to brain damage. His physical care was also becoming increasingly demanding. Getting him showered was a two and a half hour exercise, and was the task I hated the most; he had a permanent urine bag but regular 'mistakes' meant I was forever being called in to clean up.

Then The Hair

Anyone who knew Mark understood his hair was one of his preoccupations — you might even say an obsession. He was pedantic about his hair, and he looked after it like a girl.

He took longer in the shower washing and conditioning his hair than I did.

As evidence of this 'hair fetish' we have a whole photo album devoted to a few days before his brain surgery when he cut off his dreads in preparation for his operation. It was a big occasion, with at least a dozen family members and close friends present to witness and take part in this historic barbering session, and we still have the shorn dreadlocks saved for posterity.

After his radiation therapy his hair never grew back the same as it had been before his illness, but he still valiantly shaped it into weird creations we referred to by 'pet' names; the sundial (one piece of hair 'gel-ed' back to look like a horn,) soon superseded by a three-hued Mohawk, followed by the blue and green Spider, a few long dreadlocks which fell either side of his face that looked like hairy spider legs.

So the day he asked me to cut his hair was a Red Letter Day in his universe. He wanted something different, but he didn't explain himself clearly, and as I was to discover, I hadn't grasped what he was trying to tell me. I shaved his head where I thought he wanted it shaved.

I have no idea what I did wrong, but to Mark it seemed I'd somehow destroyed an important part of his identity. I found him sobbing in the shower because he said I had cut his hair wrong. Just prior to getting into the shower he'd stripped naked with the bedroom door wide open before I'd got his towel or robe ready for him — behavior that was completely out of character for a Dad who was always concerned about being modest and appropriate with four daughters in the house.

It seemed the Mark we knew was disintegrating in front of our eyes. I didn't recognize the man he was becoming, and I found it increasingly difficult to relate to this Mark; he was not the man I had known. I missed the companionship of our marriage, and I was already grieving the loss of the beloved husband I knew. He'd been stolen by illness.

He depended on me for everything, yet when it suited him he seemed perfectly capable of getting what he wanted for himself. What I had was not a husband, but rather a fifth child. Even more distressing, the older girls were noticing these changes and had started to mock or disobey him.

I wrestled constantly with thoughts of Mark's illness being over and not having to look after a sick man anymore. I just wanted to get on with my life, but at the same time struggled with the knowledge of how much I would miss Mark; I understood I already missed 'my Mark.' I felt so many conflicting emotions. I kept praying that my eyes might be kept on Jesus, who in Hebrews 12:2 speaks about being the 'author and perfecter of faith.'

I had no idea how to pray other than beg God for this to be over; either heal Mark or take him home to heaven, but please end this illness. I found comfort in Romans 8:26–28, 'Meanwhile the moment we get tired of waiting, God's Spirit is right alongside helping us along. If we don't know how or what to pray, it doesn't matter. He does our praying in and for us, making prayer out of our wordless sighs, our aching groans. He knows us far better than we know ourselves, knows our pregnant condition, and keeps us present before God. That's why we can be sure that every detail in our lives of love for God is worked into something good' (MSG).

We were increasingly enveloped in a fog of despair. I frequently felt that life didn't make any sense. I had bound every cancer cell in Mark's body to the will of God and the scary thing was we couldn't see any change. Job 14:14, 18–19 states, 'All through these difficult days I keep hoping, waiting for the final change – for resurrection! . . . Meanwhile mountains wear down and boulders break up, stones wear smooth and soil erodes as you relentlessly grind down our hope' (MSG).

I asked myself whether the Lord grinds down our hope in very earthly carnal things because He wants to replace it with hope in Him and His concerns. As I look back, I saw Mark and I had lots of hope in what we wanted to do for God in the future. Now, a few years into this, we just hoped in God.

Wrong Change

I had prayed for change, but when it came in the form of a new diagnosis, we were both completely shattered. For me, the day of the new diagnosis was a game changer. It was the day I really began questioning what faith was all about. The day I started down a very lonely path of self-discovery. After a routine MRI— to see how far the tumor had progressed— we were told Mark was severely brain damaged from the radiation treatment he had received, but the tumor was apparently gone. Some might have considered this great news; Mark's tumor was no longer evident, and the 'collateral damage' of permanent disability, a small price to pay.

But the realization that any sort of recovery was unlikely was a bitter pill to swallow. Mark was now permanently disabled by radiation necrosis, a rare side effect of radiotherapy, something the experts told us occurred in only 0.1 percent of cases.

It dawned on me that this latest cataclysm had been delivered three years to the day after we'd received Mark's original diagnosis. So when I had heard 'three years' when walking out of the oncologist's office back in June 2000, God must have been preparing me for this turning point. I had taken it to mean 'three years and this will be over.' My hearing God's voice was right, but my interpretation of the implication was so very wrong. He might not die from this cancer after all, but he could, probably would, live on for an indeterminate number of years growing increasingly disabled. For both of us, this was the worst possible news.

CHAPTER FOUR
TAKING A LOOK IN THE MIRROR

'Head, if you cross that line, you can never go back.'
- Roadie to Brian Welch.

HEAVY METAL rocker-turned born-again Christian Brian 'Head' Welch from the band Korn has recently spoken about the capacity of anyone to make bad choices under the weight of heavy circumstances. He was commenting on the 2014 conviction and six-year-jail term handed down to *As I Lay Dying* heavy metal singer Tim Lambesis for attempting to hire a hit man to murder his wife. Lambesis had apparently often quoted a line from the Arnold Schwarzenegger movie *Total Recall* when Schwarzenegger, playing construction worker Douglas Quaid, shoots his supposed wife Sharon Stone and says, 'Consider that a divorce.'

Head recalled an out-of-control, drug-addled evening when, high as a kite on cocaine he had asked a roadie with gang connections what it would take to have his wife and her new boyfriend 'hurt really bad or worse. . .' Fortunately for Welch, the roadie countered with; 'Head if you cross that line, you can never go back,' and he took the impulse no further.

In a candid post on his popular monthly column on Loudwire, Head commented that the sentence Lambesis was facing 'could have been me.' He continued: 'Some people can handle more or less than others, but EVERYONE has a certain breaking point — especially if there are other substances involved.' (Lambesis blamed his skewed judgment on heavy steroid use.) Welch titled the piece 'Taking a Look in The Mirror.'

What I became as Mark's illness progressed helped me understand what Welch was talking about, because in my mounting anguish for some resolution of Mark's situation, I grew increasingly desperate. I was so sick of my heart hurting, so sick of watching my family try and cope as Mark got sicker and sicker. And if — like Brian Welch — I looked in a mirror, I was humbled at where my extreme reactions were taking me. What I saw reflected left me shame-faced at how harshly I sometimes treated Mark. In my desolation, I teetered on the edge of doing him physical harm.

God revealed, during my early morning scripture time, my growing feelings of bitterness towards Mark. This was not something I had recognised in myself, but as soon as the Lord highlighted it, I realized it was true. I forgave Mark when he asked me to, but increasingly the hurt was caused by things he wasn't conscious of or couldn't control.

Before I knew it, I was carrying a big mountain of hurt and unforgiveness. My prayer became, 'I am so sorry God! Thank you Lord for showing me this. Help me to truly forgive Mark for all the hurt. I can say I forgive him but I know the hurt goes deep and so the cleansing needs to go deep too.' I prayed out loud from Psalm 51:10, 'Create in me a clean heart, O God. Renew a loyal spirit within me.'

God also spoke to me clearly one day through Matthew 12:34–37, 'You brood of snakes! How could evil men like you speak what is good and right? For whatever is in your heart determines what you say. A good person produces good things from the treasury of a good heart, and an evil person produces evil things from the treasury of an evil heart. And I tell you this, you must give an account on judgment day for every idle word you speak. The words you say will either acquit you or condemn you.'

I knew the Lord was giving me a good telling off and I fully deserved it. I had an evil and unforgiving heart towards Mark and had spoken angry hurtful words to him. I made excuses like 'I am tired' and 'it's not fair' and 'I want my old husband.' But there were no excuses. I needed to ask forgiveness from the Lord and Mark, and I needed to forgive Mark. That was all there was to it!

Year Of Miracle Healing

I look back on 2006 as the 'The Year of Miracle Healing.' Not because it happened, but because I poured so much energy into trying to make it happen. However, it didn't begin that way. I was so exhausted by the well-meaning suggestions of others. Early that year when a woman in the church told me she and another church elder really believed Mark was going to be healed, I just felt really angry.

Our days were dictated by Mark's illness and many of our typical days were hard, sad days. Mark would have a three hour seizure, horrible fits where he was conscious but couldn't control his body and was in a lot of pain. He thrashed around out of control, arms wheeling and head lolling, involuntarily making awful noises.

These frightening turns were disturbing for us all to witness. He also endured constant pain and vomiting. It was dreadful watching him brace his head in his arms because of the severe pain while we went madly scampering for the morphine. Living with this grim daily reality, I had little patience with glib declarations of 'God's healing.'

It was fine and dandy for people to thoughtlessly make statements like that, I reflected, but it just rubbed salt into the wounds I was carrying from caring for Mark for the last five or six years, and they should keep their annoying opinions to themselves. However, a surprise phone call from Atilla Abricoso, a very old friend in Australia, changed my attitude almost overnight.

We had known Atilla for many years in our local church, First Presbyterian Papakura, before he moved across the Tasman. Our church had been like a big family of 300 plus people. Although we hadn't really heard from him in years and he was older than Mark and me, we still regarded him as kin and trusted him. We knew him to be kind and genuine.

He said he was just ringing out of the blue because he had been healed, and he'd seen many other people healed through the teaching in a book called *Healing the Sick,* by T. L. (Tommy Lee) Osborn, an American Pentecostal evangelist whose ministry emphasized God's love and compassion. Lee was said to have seen frequent evidence of supernatural healings in his meetings.

The very randomness of Atilla's reappearance in our lives might have been partly behind my impulsive acceptance. There had been many calls like his over the years since Mark's diagnosis, and normally we just ignored them, but I was intrigued by the excitement in Atilla's voice. He wasn't judging or being critical; I felt he genuinely cared for Mark and was offering us hope.

I had also been noticing a verse in Hosea 4:6 that seemed to keep popping up in my Bible reading which says, 'My people are destroyed for lack of knowledge.' When Atilla quoted this very same verse, he got my attention.

I had started to wonder if indeed we were lacking in understanding about biblical teaching on healing. I agreed to read the book if he sent it. Perhaps in my desperation I was scared that I'd 'missed the boat' for Mark. Maybe God still did really want to heal him and we'd failed to do our part by not praying enough, or expressing our faith for healing enough, or not having a clear enough understanding of the way God's healing power worked.

Wishful Thinking?

Surfing a new wave of hope, I allowed myself to believe again that God was going to heal Mark. And I carried Mark along with me. We encouraged ourselves with faith building verses like those from Romans 10:17, 'Faith comes by listening to this message of good news...' Exodus 23:25 caught my attention, 'You must serve only the Lord your God. If you do, I will bless you with food and water and I will protect you from illness.' As well as Exodus 15:26, 'I am the Lord who heals you.'

We strove to see God's working with the eyes and mind of a child. We prayed together for Mark's complete healing. Mark fasted, and I felt a keen anticipation about how wonderful it was going to be to see my darling husband healed.

The two things that really impacted me as I read Osborn's book were his interpretation of scripture and his emphasis that first, when asking God to forgive my sins, it never occurred to me that He won't or He hasn't. It says in the scriptures that He forgives when we ask and I have asked, so I know He has, there is no doubt. Why don't I feel the same way about the scriptures that promise healing? And secondly, God indubitably loves us with a Father's love. He doesn't want this illness on us. As we want the best for Misha, Bonnie, Jasmine and Emerald, so God wants the best for us.

With these and many other supportive scriptures in our hearts we anticipated Mark's health being fully restored. I kept expecting to turn around and see it happen. In my precious prayer time I'd say to the Lord, 'When you heal Mark, it is going to be so cool. People will see this miracle and turn to you. Mark and I will be able to lead so many people to you because they will know you are still the miracle-working God. I will be able to lead them to a God who not only is our strength and comfort, but a God who can heal.'

As my thirty-sixth birthday arrived, I begged God for the present of Mark's complete healing and restoration. My faith was certain God would and could do this, and we waited with such excitement. And God led me to Isaiah 64:3–4, which gave me encouragement. Isaiah notes, 'When you came down long ago, you did awesome deeds beyond our highest expectations. And oh, how the mountains quaked! For since the world began, no ear has heard and no eye has seen a God like you, who works for those who wait for him!'

My prayers were, 'How fabulous you are Lord! Please use this power to finish Mark's healing quickly, in Jesus' name.' But as the months rolled by and a few promising signs of improvement evaporated, I felt waves of sadness washing over me. Was this really what life was going to be about? I really did have the faith to believe for Mark's healing, but it wasn't happening in any way we could comprehend.

I had started to get excited again about what the future would hold for us when Mark was well. I wanted to travel and show the girls the world. I wanted a husband who was well, and once again I wanted to be the one who was looked after and cared for. Instead, I was stuck in New Zealand doing nothing exciting, looking after an invalid husband who didn't seem to be receiving healing.

A month later in my early morning time with the Lord I was led to Psalm 18:30, 'God's way is perfect. All the Lord's promises prove true. He is a shield for all who look to Him for protection.' This was interesting; God was reminding me His ways are perfect! Not just okay or good or even great, but perfect! I remembered God teaching me about His promises a few years before and now was reminded again.

I was reading John Bevere's book, *Driven by Eternity* (Warner Faith) and in it I was discovering more scriptures on obedience and how it brings abundant life. I had also started listening to John Bevere on TV, and he was teaching on obedience and blessing. I felt like I was being obedient praying and believing for healing even if it didn't happen.

But I could see God was teaching me about more than healing. By mid-August there was still no change in Mark's illness. I was feeling submerged in sorrow; there had been no healing yet. God was in control and like Job, though I didn't understand, who was I to question? I kept on trusting and having faith to believe the Bible which is God's 'living and active word' (Hebrews 4:12).

As 2007 began and Mark was showing signs of further mental as well as physical deterioration, I resolved to revert to coping one day at a time and roll with the punches. I decided that mostly the year would be one focused on enjoying my girls, the greatest gift God had given me. Misha, (now thirteen) was as tall as me; twelve-year-old Bonnie had such a love for life; Jasmine, nearly ten, saw life so differently from me, and Emerald (eight) was always going to be my baby no matter how big she grew.

I took comfort in James 5:11 and thanked God for the promise of a good ending, 'We give great honor to those who endure under suffering. Job is an example of a man who endured patiently. From his experience we see how the Lord's plan finally ended in good, for he is full of tenderness and mercy.'

Effectively being a solo parent of four teenagers was definitely not what I had planned and it was hard to come to terms with it, as Mark, in normal health, would have made the best Dad of teenagers. Apparently though, 'I can do all things through Christ who gives me the strength I need' (Phil. 4:13). 'Love never gives up, never loses faith, is always hopeful and endures through every circumstance' (1 Cor. 13:7).

CHAPTER FIVE
GOD, WHY DON'T YOU HEAL MARK?

'It would be so nice if something made sense for a change …'- Alice in *Alice in Wonderland* - Lewis Carroll.

BENNY HINN is a tele-evangelist, best known for his regular 'Miracle Crusades'— faith healing summits usually held at stadiums in major cities, and later broadcast worldwide on his television program, *This Is Your Day.* I didn't have a particularly high opinion of his ministry from the TV shows, which seemed sensational and focused on making Benny Hinn a star. In normal circumstances, I would not have considered attending his crusades in a million years. But in July 2007, I found out by chance that he was speaking in Auckland. I impulsively loaded everyone into our van and off we went.

When I considered my motives later I guess it was a mixture of:

- ☐ A man with a renowned healing ministry is here
- ☐ Maybe God is going to heal Mark through him
- ☐ I am willing to try anything. I would kick myself if somehow this was our opportunity and we missed it

It was like I was 'ticking things off a list.' I definitely knew I had the faith for Mark to be healed, and I wanted to be sure I had tried everything. It was an amazing evening, although nothing like I had presumed from watching him on TV. There is a flashiness on his TV shows that wasn't there in reality. The sensationalism that is portrayed on the TV shows where he is loud and center stage — it just wasn't like that at all. The worship was wonderful; God's presence was there, and we watched as people did appear to get healed.

We were totally expectant that this was going to be Mark's night — but it wasn't. And I hadn't fully taken into consideration the impact that would have on the girls as they watched others get out of their wheelchairs, but not their Dad. They got extremely upset. I tried to get them to focus on the fact others were being healed. Although it sucked that it wasn't Mark, we needed to still praise God for the healings we did witness.

Amazingly enough, they all seemed to grasp that and shared the joy that others around us were experiencing. I was so involved in helping my girls through the experience of their hopes being dashed all over again that I didn't have any time for introspection about my own response to this latest disappointment.

Life Gets Weirder

Like a delayed concussion, the 'Hinn hangover' struck me like a tsunami in the days after the crusade. I found myself stretched beyond my ability to cope. I was bad tempered, tired, and the slightest incident sent me into a rage or dissolved into tears.

It was so bad that one morning I lost my temper because we hadn't eaten all the porridge I had cooked for breakfast: I just saw money going down the waste disposal unit. I lost it again at Mark for not noticing the cat needed feeding. On the fourth night after our crushing disappointment, I felt incandescent with anger and desperation. I became so terrified of my own feelings and what I might be capable of doing; I didn't trust myself to go to bed alongside Mark.

I truly thought I might do him physical harm. I was so freaked out by my thoughts; I lay on the lounge room couch, with my hands pinned underneath me. Talk about 'there but for the grace of God go I.' I knew I loved Mark. I knew I didn't want to hurt him. And yet I was having thoughts of going to the kitchen and getting a knife to stab him. I had never felt anything like this before, and I couldn't believe it was happening to me.

I lay on that couch and prayed to God all night that I wouldn't hurt Mark physically or emotionally. I was just so tired of the sickness. Seeing people healed at the Hinn crusade seemed to be the final straw. Mark wasn't healed — again. 'God, why isn't it good enough for you to heal Mark when you healed those other people?'

My thoughts strayed back to the months before Mark got ill. It is April 2000 and Mark is well and still has his long dreads and is working hard. He is a wonderful loving attentive husband and my girls have their cool Daddy back.

I recall the words in the Lord's Prayer in Matthew 6:10, 'Your kingdom come, your will be done on earth as it is in heaven.' And I pray, 'Lord, make me want your will. I want this to be over, so you have to make me want your will. Change my heart. Help me Lord, I am desperate. I need you to move miraculously and change me because I seriously hate this. Help me!'

Sometime in the early hours of that dreadful morning, I looked to 1 John 3:10, 15, 18–20, 'Anyone who does not obey God's commands and does not love other Christians does not belong to God. . . Anyone who hates another Christian is really a murderer at heart. . . Dear children, let us stop just saying we love each other, let us really show it by our actions. It is by our actions that we know we are living in the truth, so we will be confident when we stand before the Lord, even if our hearts condemn us. For God is greater than our hearts and he knows everything.'

I found it reassuring and releasing to know that God knew exactly what was in my heart. And He didn't say to me, 'Suz, it's okay that you had those terrible hateful thoughts last night because it is so hard doing what you are doing.' No. God actually said to me that if I hate, I am a murderer at heart.

I have to love Mark and show it by my actions so I can confidently stand before Jesus. 'I'm so sorry Lord for my hateful thoughts last night – it was extreme and it truly scared me. Thank you for getting me through the night and for now giving me a kick up the butt with this scripture.'

The whole episode was way outside any 'normal' boundaries of my experience; it felt like an outright spiritual attack. So it really came as no surprise when Emerald woke and told me she had a very strange dream of red snakes attacking us during the night. I felt gratitude all over again that God was showing me the intensely negative feelings I had experienced were from a spiritual attack.

And I was incredibly grateful I had been able to pray my way through them and not act on them. I texted a small group of my closest friends and asked them to pray for us and to protect me and the house from further attacks. And I spent the following day with worship music playing very loudly in the house, just praying for God to be present and sovereign and for Satan to flee, since he had no authority there.

'I' The Problem

I knew this was a very unusual experience, and that there were spiritual forces at work. I also had to face up to some unpalatable realities. I realized the biggest issue, if I was truly honest with myself and God, was me.

I was making the experience all about me: 'It's so hard for me to look after a sick husband.' 'It's so hard on me raising my girls alone.' 'It's so hard on me having to do all the housework, all the gardening, all the everything around the home. I want to feel loved again.' 'I want to be provided for.' 'I want Mark to be well again, or a new husband.' 'I want, I want, I want!'

I had brought on the attack from Satan by my own selfishness. Oh my goodness what a realization. Me! I understood I had to take me out of the equation, and put Jesus back in his rightful place of first in my life. I must then put Mark and the girls before me. I must take up this cross, Mark's illness and all that comes with it. I must deny myself! In my journal I noted verses from Isaiah 63 that describe how God tramples on His enemies.

I felt God was saying He had trampled on the selfishness and self-centeredness that had led to my rage. I recorded my conclusions, 'I've learned a whole lot from the last twenty-four hours:

1. My actions, attitude and selfishness cause a whole lot of trouble and allow Satan access to me and my home.

2. God does not muck around in telling me it is my fault, and for that I am so grateful.

3. God is then so gracious, He forgives when we are repentant and then He comes and cleans up the mess.'

I was overwhelmed by the whole experience. How humbling it was that after exposing the depravity in my own heart and realizing how revolting I would be without Jesus and His grace and forgiveness, I still got to speak with others and share my story about what God has done for us.

And I still believed God was going to use me to share all that He was teaching me, to show others how God wanted to be involved in every area of our lives whether good, bad and even horrible. God had walked with me these seven years, and I still wanted to tell everyone how amazing He was.

CHAPTER SIX
LORD, WHERE ELSE COULD WE GO?

'Fifty years from now, when you're looking back at your life, don't you want to be able to say you had the guts to get in the car?' - Sam Witwicky, *Transformers*.

IN A FAMOUS showdown in the movie *Transformers,* hero Sam Witwicky's (Shia LaBeouf's) car turns into the autobot, Bumble Bee, and has an epic fight with a Decepticon. Once the duel is over, Bumble Bee transforms back into a car and drives up to Sam and Mikaela Banes (Megan Fox) and opens his door as an invitation to them to get in. Sam and Mikaela stand staring, not really sure whether it's safe to accept. Sam says to Mikaela, 'don't you want to say fifty years from now that you had the guts to get in the car!'

God often speaks to me in crazy ways and I felt Him challenge me about accepting this situation, and the calling or mission that came with it. It was like *Transformers* — 'don't say fifty years from now you didn't have the guts to go on with me.' I felt the challenge to have the courage to live this life well, to trust God with my future and then to have fortitude to make a difference with what God was teaching us, hoping we could also communicate it to other people and make a difference in their lives.

After all the years of seeking healing from God for Mark, and it not happening in any way we could see with our eyes, and all the craziness of cancer tumors, radiation necrosis, the constant financial challenges, I felt the Lord was still asking me: 'Do you trust me Suz?' And I could still reply, 'You know what – yes Lord, I do accept this and yes as crazy as it seems, even with what I've experienced the last eight years, I do trust you. I accept because I do not want to get to eternity and see what I missed out on. I don't want to get to heaven and find there are people who aren't there because I didn't accept this challenge and this calling today.

'I want to be able to say I had the guts to say "Yes" to God when He called. I know, God, that every person on this planet has a calling, every person has the opportunity to say "Yes God" and yet not every person does. But today I say "Yes, YES LORD. I accept the calling and whatever cost, sacrifice, courage and strength I need for it. I am yours Jesus, let's go!"'

Difference With Jesus

In the midst of these difficult times, a friend rang one night and we had a long talk about the hard journeys many of us go through in life. I shared with her that although I wished none of this illness had ever happened, I didn't actually regret what we'd gone through because of what the Lord had done in my life and how much my relationship with Him had grown.

My friend was stunned. She had lost a husband to cancer and she said she totally wished that it had never happened, and she regretted the whole thing. For the first time I clearly saw the difference between doing this with God and doing this without Him.

With Him – I felt I had hope, purpose, a destiny. With Him we had the promise that He was working even this situation into something good, that we had a future. With Him we had the promise of protection, provision, comfort and wisdom. With Him we had love.

As it says in Colossians 2:7, 'Let your roots grow down into him and draw up nourishment from him, so you will grow in faith, strong and vigorous in the truth you were taught. Let your lives overflow with thanksgiving for all he has done.' And I can say 'truly Lord, I will try and overflow with thanks for all you have done in my life, especially through Mark's illness.'

I had believed without doubt that God could and would heal Mark, and yet Mark was not healed. In fact, his condition deteriorated, especially mentally. I had walked through scriptures of healing, then obedience, and then God's love, and lastly forgiveness and God's mercy. What did the Lord finish on? He finished by reminding me this is a season that my family and I have to live through, but to 'wait patiently and be brave and courageous' (Psalm 27:14).

Perhaps Mark's healing was not to be part of our story. Perhaps Mark being ill and our family choosing to still serve God is our story. Perhaps his healing will happen in a few months or a few years. Maybe he will never be healed and this is it. Or maybe he will die. I did not know; I am not God. I do know believing for Mark's healing had to be part of our journey. I do know that God required me to be obedient to His word even when I really didn't want to be obedient. And somehow in all the hurt and rage we find God in the mystery.

I do know that God loves me with an everlasting love that I don't deserve and that He has forgiven all our sins. And I do know that without God I would be a very nasty, angry and broken person. I didn't understand Him – I never have and I doubt I ever will. He allows my heart to be broken and demands obedience, while at the same time surrounds me with His love and presence. I didn't know what the future held for Mark, me and the girls, but I did know that God had told me to wait patiently and be brave and courageous.

And I knew I wanted to continue to try and live this life as well as I could. Without God I would run away. I would be weak, pathetic, selfish and cowardly. And so I choose this; I choose Jesus because no matter what God allows in my life, where else would I go? As Peter says in John 6:68, 'Simon Peter answered him, "Lord, to whom shall we go? You have the words of eternal life' (NIV). I'm with Peter on that.

PART II–
MAD AT GOD

Finding peace in painful circumstances did not come easily.

For nearly two years Suz boiled over with 'justified rage.'

We turn back the clock to ask :

'Can God handle our honesty even if other people can't?'

2003 – 2004

CHAPTER SEVEN
THE GAME CHANGER

'I was mad at God. And if people told me you can't or shouldn't be mad at God I was angry at them too.' - Suz Holmes.

MARK ALWAYS said that being a Christian is not an insurance policy against bad things happening. In 2003, the day the cancer specialist sat across from us and gently explained Mark had permanent brain scarring, but no tumor, was one of those days. I was shocked all over again that we didn't have that insurance policy.

All our faith, all our prayer, was not going to save us from having to complete this journey, however torturous. Perhaps there would be no reprieve, no miracle rescue, no convenient escape. Maybe we were going to have to walk it out for however long it took.

I felt like an unexploded grenade had been lobbed into the small sterilized anonymous clinic where we'd been summoned to receive an update on Mark's condition. If I speak, I thought then, I may detonate it . . . The tumor's absence should have been good news — evidence of a cure! Hallelujah! But instead, I was aware of a growing feeling of horror.

Mark's frequent seizures, constant pain, his inability to shower or feed himself, were all because of one six week course of radiation three years ago? I hesitated before asking the crucial question, 'And the scarring will possibly continue to grow?'

'It's likely, possible even . . . but very slowly.' Dr. Harvey seemed to be choosing his words carefully.

'And they think the tumor has not grown . . . they think the tumor has vanished?'

As I asked this question, the reality of what the doctor was saying was finally sinking in.

'They can't see any evidence of the tumor growing. No. They can't see any tumor.'

I asked the next question hesitantly, the tears already stinging my eyes.

'Can he die from scarring?'

Dr. Harvey paused for a moment, 'I suppose the answer to that is yes.'

'So he could be like this for years?'

'It's possible, although, ah . . .' I remember Dr. Harvey searching desperately for the right words, the least upsetting phrase . . . 'generally we would think, that there is . . . we would still believe there is likely to be a tumor in there, and that sooner or later the tumor will grow, even though it is too small now to see and too small to be causing most of these problems.'

I've watched myself many times on the TV documentary that was being filmed at this consultation — the documentary which was intended to record Mark's and my faith journey through this dark time. But suddenly, the documentary was not following the anticipated script.

This is what the documentary recorded: My hands go through my hair as my head drops and the tears fall. It has taken only seconds for me to understand what the doctor is telling us means for our lives. My darling Mark is not going to die. He is going to live on and on, just half the man I married . . .

'You must think this is terrible that I am crying, but I have to look after him,' I manage to croak. I point to my husband of thirteen years in his wheelchair, also stunned at the news we have just received. He is overweight, his face swollen from the heavy steroid dose he has been on to reduce the swelling around what now appears to be the non-existent tumor. He is looking from me to Dr. Harvey and back to me again.

'It's a lot of bloody hard work, and to think that I could have years of this.' There's a long, tense silence.

'Why did they never warn us, why did they never say scarring could do this? These last three years I have watched his health deteriorate thinking it was the tumor growing. What if the scarring stops and he is left like this forever?'

Dr. Harvey answers hesitantly, 'It's unlikely the scarring will stop. . .' He pauses, seemingly uncertain how to continue . . .

'But scarring doesn't get worse as quickly as the tumor gets worse, nothing as quickly.'

For a time no one speaks. I sit with my head in my hands, sobbing. At thirty-three, Mark has just been sentenced to a lifetime of terrible debilitating illness, and I, at thirty-two, have been condemned to a lifetime of caring for him.

No one can say how long that is going to be. The prison doors slam shut around us as we sit in the Auckland Hospital Oncology Department. I had forgotten about the cameraman filming the appointment.

Mark and I had agreed to take part in the documentary as part of an *Inside New Zealand* TV series, financed by the government-funded New Zealand on Air agency and planned for primetime screening. Director Rob Harley was a Television New Zealand current affairs journalist who was well known for his integrity and strong portfolio; producer Lisa Walker was a close friend. The goal was to recount our family's journey dealing with a malignant brain tumor, facing possible death, and how our Christian faith worked through it all.

Now, despite the camera, I can't stop crying. I can barely look at the cameraman as he prepares to leave with us. In silence I help Mark into the car, slowly put his wheelchair in the trunk and settle behind the wheel for the thirty minute drive home. Neither of us speaks. We are both in shock.

Our New Reality

By the time we are on the freeway heading home, my stunned tears have dissolved into white hot uncontrolled rage. I am furious! What the hell! I cannot believe this is the hand we have been dealt. Mark and Suzanne, missionaries who dedicated our lives to Jesus. Mark and Suzanne, who owned nothing because nothing was of value compared to telling people about the saving grace of Jesus. Mark and Suzanne, who have tried to do everything right our entire lives; never drank alcohol, never did drugs, never slept around, never had an affair. This is what life has handed us in return?

Then my anger turned on Mark, after all it is his head that is growing this f#*kin radiation necrosis. I start screaming at him; 'This is not what I f#*kin signed up for when I married you. You know how I feel about long-term illness. I cannot believe I am stuck with you. This f#*kin sucks!'

The one and only other time in my life I had said the 'f word' was when I was thirteen years old, and I said it in front of my cousin and her friend in the garden at home. Unfortunately for me, my dad heard it. Without hesitation, he came out of the house and administered a short, sharp dose of corporal punishment and I'd never said that word again – until now.

The ride home from the hospital seemed the perfect time for it to become part of my vocabulary again. The anger inside me was so overwhelming, the 'f word' is the only word I can think of to even slightly express the all-consuming rage I felt. Thirty minutes is a long time to have abuse hurled at you, but Mark had nowhere to escape, so he had to sit and listen. Even I could not believe the foulness that was coming out of my mouth. Suzanne, the good Christian woman, am I really capable of this ugly profanity? Apparently I am.

At home waiting for us was our dear friend Belinda Partridge who had been babysitting our four daughters. At the time Misha was nine, Bonnie was eight, Jasmine was six and Emerald was four. As I manoeuvre Mark from the car back into his wheelchair, I think to myself, 'Oh my goodness is this what I am going to have to do for years to come?' The girls rush out of the house to greet us and Emerald jumps on Mark's knee for a ride on his wheelchair, a favorite pastime for her, and one that I now despise because I am the one pushing the chair.

Belinda asks: 'How did it go?'

I don't need any further invitation.

'You are never going to believe this. It's scarring! Mark is brain damaged from the radiation. He has what is called radiation necrosis, an apparently very rare reaction to the radiation therapy used on his brain to kill the remaining cancer that was left after surgery. And what's worse, this is permanent and long-term, very long-term.' I sat on the couch in shocked silence. Belinda handed Mark and me a coffee, and then we just sat and stared into a void.

The phone rang. Belinda answered it.

'It is the TV doco producer Lisa Walker.'

'We have all just watched the filming Suz, how are you?'

'Not good Lisa, we are in shock and don't understand how this could have happened.'

'Shall I come over?' she asks.

'No, there is nothing you can do Lisa, thank you though.'

An hour or so passed and the front door opened. Standing there was Rob Harley with his hands full of cans of Dr Pepper for Mark and chocolate bars for me. 'I just couldn't stay away,' he says. The scene as it played out in the doctor's surgery has upset them all.

As Rob sat with us, I was overwhelmed that other people got it, got that this was the worst news we could have received. I'm convinced others wouldn't understand the fact that Mark's tumor appeared to have gone is not good news. Compared to this life sentence, dying now seems easy.

There will be no end for Mark; no end to the pain, the three different kinds of seizures, the incontinence, the inability to shower, shave and dress himself. There will be no end to the reliance on others to do everything for him, no end to the headaches, the terrible vision, and the complete uselessness of the right side of his body.

There is now no end to his slow and sometimes confused speech, his mind getting things all muddled, his sadness and his frustration. There is no end! And because there is no end for him, there is now no end for me.

How did this become our life? What happened to the two young missionaries who got married at a ridiculously early age and who made the most of every opportunity that God brought along? This life we are now facing couldn't be more opposite to the life we were living just a few short years ago.

CHAPTER EIGHT
OUR ROAD TO HAPPY EVER AFTER

'All we have to decide is what to do with the time that is given to us.' - Gandalf the Grey, *Lord of the Rings, Fellowship of the Ring.*

MARK AND I met in 1987 at a church youth group in suburban Auckland, New Zealand. I was sixteen, had just finished high school and had started work as a bank teller. I regarded the job as a stepping stone towards my real passion — to serve God full-time on the mission field. The youth group was planning a trip to a wild west Auckland surfing beach. We hoped to combine having normal teenage fun with 'witnessing' — talking about Jesus with the holidaymakers who flocked to the coast on hot summer's days.

Mark was a year older than me, and had just arrived back from Tonga where his family had been working with Youth With A Mission (YWAM). It wasn't 'love at first sight,' that's for sure. I thought he was a bit of a 'nerd,' but he was a nice nerd, and he had a passion for missions which was totally where my heart lay. We became friends and got on really well. He had a great sense of humor, was easy going and got along with everyone. It didn't take him long to become part of the youth group and establish firm friendships with us all.

And that could have been that. At the end of the summer, Mark went to Amsterdam with his parents, David and Val, and his younger brother Phillip, where David and Val were taking part in a six month YWAM Leadership Training School. He returned a year later looking anything but nerdy. I sat up and took notice. His short, curly, mousy brown hair was now bright red and shaved in amazing patterns at the back and sides. He was growing his front bangs out long like heavy metal rocker Eddie Van Halen. He wore tight black ripped jeans, high top Converse sneakers and a long black trench coat. He had five earrings in one ear and one in the other. My indifference evaporated. He'd gotten my attention.

We officially started 'going out' on June 7th 1988. Mark was eighteen and I was three weeks shy of eighteen. Because Mark had lived overseas until recently, he hadn't got his driver's license, so we couldn't go on 'traditional' dates unless we persuaded my dad or a friend to drive us somewhere.

Mark was also broke and jobless; he had tried hairdressing, but got bad dermatitis from the shampoos, and he was on an unemployment benefit. That didn't matter to me. He was generous with what he did have, which was time and a bicycle. Most days he came to my house for dinner and stayed for the evening and then biked home. There was a round-about in the street not far from my house and on his way home Mark would pick wild flowers from it, bike back and give them to me through my bedroom window. I thought he was wonderful.

At the beginning of 1989, Mark and I decided to spend two months with his parents, assisting in building a new YWAM Discipleship Training School in Tonga. It was there on a moonlit, palm tree-silhouetted waterfront that Mark got down on one knee and proposed marriage. We'd been dating for seven months, and of course I said 'Yes'.

I was convinced even before we had started dating that Mark was 'the one' God had chosen for me to marry because of a vision I had when we were still just good buddies. In my fervent determination to put every life decision under God's guidance, I'd been praying about what place — if any — Mark had in my life.

As I prayed, I saw myself as a twelve year old standing by a book shelf in a classroom I recognized as my old school. Like a movie unfolding I saw myself pray, 'God, don't ever let me have a boyfriend unless it's the guy you want me to marry.' Then in the vision I saw big hands materialize in front of my twelve-year-old self.

With a sweeping motion, the hands pushed aside boys I recognized were young men I had felt attracted to during my teenage years, or boys who had fancied me. Then the hands paused and gestured with an open-handed motion towards Mark.

I felt a strong impression that this was the guy that God had chosen for me. It seemed to flash past in seconds, but when it was over I immediately remembered praying that twelve-year-old's prayer, a memory I had forgotten until then. And it made me understand why I had never had a boyfriend in my school years. I was thinking I must be ugly and that when my parents reassured me I was beautiful, they were just being loving parents.

Now Mark had confirmed I was desirable and he wanted me as his wife. Our joy at our engagement was met with equal enthusiasm by Mark's parents, who were thrilled at the prospect of having me as a daughter-in-law.

Not so, my Mum and Dad however; they cried at our news, and it was not from happiness. They did not consider Mark ideal fiancée material for their one and only daughter. They saw an out-of-work would-be rock musician who wore outlandish clothes and wasn't much of a prospect as a 'steady provider.' He'd adopted the 'metal band' style of black for everything. He had even painted perfectly respectable shoes black.

If he did wear blue jeans, they were ripped and shredded. His red hair had been replaced by a jet black dye job and his bangs were still only half-way grown out — and a curly mess. We were all into heavy music and all the musicians from the well-known bands had long hair, so we were all trying for the same look. He sported multiple earrings, sometimes wore eyeliner, played electric guitar very heavy and very loud and the icing on the cake, he was unemployed.

His outrageous get-up frightened some people, who crossed the road to avoid him, but I saw the nicest, kindest guy I had ever met. He loved Jesus and wanted to spend his life serving God. He was not at all materialistic, and he was passionate about all music and using it to reach people with the truth and gospel of Jesus. I adored him.

We married eleven months after that Tongan proposal on December 9, 1989. My parents had said they would only give their blessing to our marriage once Mark had found a job. We might have considered ourselves convention-challenging would-be rock musicians, but we had the most traditional wedding imaginable.

We exchanged our vows to 'love, honor and obey, till death do us part' in front of 230 guests. Both our mothers wore hats at my insistence. The girl who wore practically nothing but black came down the aisle on her Father's arm in a white satin and lace wedding dress with a long train, attended by two bridesmaids also in white. The groom and groomsmen were all in formal suits with red cummerbunds. Mark was twenty and I was nineteen; the guests almost died of shock.

Happy Decade

If the guests were surprised at the orthodox caste of our wedding ceremony, Mark and I were perturbed to find our first few months of married life weren't all cosiness and bliss. We discovered that while we might share common values, temperamentally we were very different.

I like everything in its place to the point of being pedantic; Mark was very laid-back and relaxed. But with love and understanding we worked out daily disciplines that suited us both. It was a bit more complicated than 'I wrote the lists of what needed to be done' and then we both worked on them, but that came close.

I was the organizer and Mark was a totally loving, hardworking and generous husband. We didn't have much in the way of material possessions, but Mark was always eager to show me in little ways that I was precious to him.

In July 1992, after a couple of years that felt like we were 'waiting for our calling to begin' we packed our bags and set off for Amsterdam to start our missionary life with YWAM's Steiger International, working as roadies with other bands while Mark continued to develop his own musical talent.

A lot of the time we were engaged in very unglamorous tasks, working till 3:00 a.m. some days loading up after gigs, but we felt we were fulfilling our destiny and we were learning so much. For the next six years we worked in Amsterdam, New Zealand

and the USA and traveled to Germany, Norway, Denmark, Sweden and Poland. Mark went to Spain and Austria as well.

Along the way we had four daughters, who joined us in our nomadic life, sleeping at my feet in the crew's Safe Zone at concerts and accepting the constant moving and changing without complaints. We couldn't have been happier doing what we had planned for all our lives.

We cherished our girls as totally gorgeous and Mark was a fabulous Dad. I remember thinking how blessed these girls were to have such a great father who adored them. Being a family was something we loved and our marriage got better and better every year.

We felt very settled with life in Houston working at Mission X with Tim Bisagno and his wife Edye, along with drummer Marty Durlam and our dear friends Stephen (bass player) and Katherine Pether from New Zealand, who we had commandeered to join us.

This team was like a family and we loved doing life with them, so it was unsettling when we felt an abrupt sense of our future direction changing. We both began feeling strongly God was calling us to provide 'stability and security' for our little family back in New Zealand.

It was a wrench for us to relinquish our Houston work and connections, particularly for Mark who was so passionate about his music. But as we looked back after Mark became ill, we realized that there was some sort of providential provision in us being home before we had to face the storm of Mark's life-threatening illness.

Thanks to the insistence of my parents, we had taken out mortgage insurance so we were settled and secure in our own house when Mark became ill. And although making ends meet was a constant financial challenge, we were a lot better off than many families faced with similar circumstances.

CHAPTER NINE
LIVING MY WORST FEAR

'It is a good thing God chose me before I was born, because he surely would not have afterwards.' - Charles Spurgeon.

THE NEWS that Mark's debilitated condition was due to a medical mishap, and the abrupt transition to my new role as a nurse/caregiver to a seriously ill husband was not one I found easy to make. For me, the prospect of living with permanent disability was a game changer. This was partly because of the disruption illness had caused in my previously happy family as I was growing up.

I was one of those incredibly fortunate children raised in a prolific Christian family. Until my mid-teens, we lived an expansive generous life, characterized by my Mother's family culture of 'Open Home, Open Heart.'

My brothers Robert, Adam and I were surrounded by loving relations. We had over thirty cousins, eighteen aunties and uncles and six grand or great-grand parents because my Mother's grandparents lived until they were 99 and 100 respectively. There was fun and love in abundance. We had the tiniest house, but it was open to anyone.

Mum had an amazing gift of hospitality, and there was always room for one more around the table. If visitors were there close to dinner time she'd just put more peas in the pot and add more chairs around the table. But that changed in my early teens when my Mother began to suffer persistent ill health. She had surgery for acute endometriosis and never fully recovered.

Mum was legitimately, seriously ill, but I hated the way illness seemed to rob her of a happy, fruitful life. It stole her ability to offer hospitality, and because of illness, my parents have not been able to travel or do many of the things I know my dad would have liked to do. I saw — and hated — the way illness could define someone. To me, illness was not who a person was, it was something they had.

This meant that I was probably the last person in the world suited to the role I now had to fulfil. I know from my journal entries that in the days leading up to the revelation that Mark was not going to die but live on permanently damaged, God had been speaking to me through the scriptures about Christian virtues that we as followers of Jesus are supposed to display. In 2 Peter 1:5 it describes those virtues, 'goodness, knowledge, self-control, godliness, kindness, love and perseverance.'

I discovered that the word perseverance was used a lot in the Bible. I also found it in Hebrews 12:1 where we are instructed to 'run the race with perseverance' — that is 'to go on doing something even though it is difficult or tedious' according to the Oxford Everyday Dictionary, (Oxford University Press 2000.)

I was trying hard to maintain a brave face, but the realization — and accompanying guilt— that I was not managing well was becoming increasingly hard to avoid. And when we were informed Mark was going to live on brain damaged, I felt myself change inside pretty much instantaneously. I began a freefall into a completely foreign and unknown realm; I entered a place I never thought I would ever go – a crisis of faith.

All my selfish passions came to the surface. I was screaming on the inside. All I had wanted was for this to be over and instead I got stuck with my worst fear – living with and caring for a sick person for the rest of my life.

Perhaps after watching my Mother with her illness and realizing the toll it took on a family, I couldn't believe that I was going to have to deal with it all over again. All I could say was, 'God I need the biggest helping of divine grace that you have.' Already I had been struggling with feelings of jealousy over my friends who had their husbands to do things with and to do the man's jobs and to go out with.

Around the time of Mark's thirty-fourth birthday in September 2003, I'd fallen apart. Distraught at my lack of feelings in my marriage, I hid from Mark in Jasmine's and Emerald's closet. I didn't want him to see me because there was nothing he could do, and I didn't want to upset him. I sat on the girls' dress-up box with the closet doors closed and wept until I had no more tears to cry. . . and then I discovered it was also a great place to pray.

I had begun nursing a secret desire for another husband – someone strong, who could do things to help me, who'd look after me, who I could cuddle up with on the couch, make love too, someone to share dreams with, even someone just to drive me places.

All the dreams I had dreamed with Mark, I had already thrown away. Now, with this new diagnosis of long-term disability, any new dreams of a new healthy husband had to be discarded too. I felt like Joseph – I had gone from slavery to a prison. It was small consolation that maybe that was where

God's greatest work in me was going to be done. Over and over in my head the selfish line played out, 'But what about me, I want to be looked after.'

Fronting Up To Necrosis

Fortunately for me, some of those closest to us also grasped the significance of the radiation necrosis diagnosis and how it changed things. Mark's parents David and Val rang one evening, and rather tentatively mentioned they were considering moving house to be closer to us. They would be able to have Mark for regular overnight stays. They were asking my permission for this move; would I feel comfortable with it?

My first reaction was to discount the idea as unnecessary and even a little smothering, but I quickly realized it was a very generous offer, and that I was going to need their help more than ever. And our very close friends Neil and Rachel Carter also quickly understood the enormity of the new situation for us.

We went to stay with them about a week after we received the new diagnosis. New Zealand schools break up for the winter holidays mid-year, so the whole family decamped to Rotorua, the city famous for its boiling hot mud pools in the central North Island where Neil and Rachel were now living.

Neil was the drummer in Mark's first band in New Zealand and also for The Friendlys when they toured NZ. He was the best man at our wedding. He'd been staunchly with us through the whole ordeal, acting as my driver when Mark was in hospital. He'd been on hand at critical moments like when Mark had his first grand mal seizure, to help us through.

He and Rachel once again stood in the gap when we most needed their devotion. In Rotorua that week we had a chance to talk openly and honestly with people who loved Mark dearly, but who were also willing to deal with what this new diagnosis meant for our future.

Chatting with Rachel I started to feel like everything was going to be okay again. As we exhaustively chewed over the whole situation, I was ready to believe all over again: The Lord has His hand in it. If this is His will I will be okay and the Lord will have to be sufficient. I release all into His hands.

I still believed that the Lord would use the girls and me to speak into the lives of many. But obviously I had to go through more, be humbled more, refined more and emptied totally. I prayed fervently, 'Lord, do what you must. I pray, please, may I glorify your name and never dishonor you.'

But now we had to face up to this new state of being permanently disabled, but not terminally ill. And the first thing we had to grapple with was the reaction of those around us to this news, which was curious and varied.

Many just didn't know what to say to us and could not find it in themselves to offer either comfort or comment. As I told and retold others of Mark's dilemma, it seemed I was repeating some kind of bad joke. I still felt like at any point I would wake up and discover it was all just a bad dream.

Mark was affected too. He became really teary, and his usual laid-back demeanor deserted him. Each time he had a bad pain, the appreciation that this state was for the long haul overwhelmed him; he understood there was no end in sight.

Every day I renewed my well-intended desire to be a loving caregiver and show Jesus through my situation, but as the days went by I acknowledged I was not coping. I felt like I was suffocating in my prison. I later understood why the fear of the Lord is the beginning of wisdom, because it was keeping me from running away and leaving all behind. My mind was a mess. I regularly pleaded, 'Oh God, I want this over, please! I am suffocating. All chance of a normal adult life is being ripped from my reach.'

In one terrible moment of venting these conflicting feelings, I told Mark that I regretted marrying him. Not the first ten years, but these last three. I couldn't believe how mean I was, but the anger was just welling up in me. Of course I apologized to him. I didn't really mean it. Talk about being afflicted.

Again I prayed, 'God, you are God. I submit to your will even though my emotions are a mess. I still submit and I still say, God, your will be done, your kingdom come on earth as it is in heaven. I am still completely your servant and I still love you and I long to glorify you. Please forgive my thoughts of escape. As I submit to you, I resist the devil and I pray that no weapon forged against me will prevail and I pray you will refute every tongue that accuses me, in Jesus' name.'

Chapter Ten
Compassion Fatigue

'Always look at what you have left. Never look at what you have lost.' - Robert H Schuller.

AS THE NEWS of Mark's necrosis spread, our wider community reacted in other interesting ways, which meant more change for us. We had been receiving meals two nights a week from people in our church for the last year and a half, which was such an incredible blessing.

Now we were told this benefit would not be continued. I could understand that now our situation was categorized as an 'indefinite suspension.' I thought people may no longer want to continue with meals on an open-ended basis, so I felt obliged to say to everyone if they wanted to stop the extra favors we had so gratefully received, I understood. But when they took me up on it, I felt alone and abandoned.

I noticed people liked to be helpful when the situation was dramatic and they could keep their finger on the pulse of the 'latest' news and 'be there' for the climax. Now that this was a long-term, possibly static condition, people were pulling away and no longer felt the desire to help. 'Charity fatigue' was something that occurred a very long way from home. Now I discovered it in my own neighborhood!

In the midst of so much darkness, there were occasional wonderful moments with the girls, who while they were normal contrary kids much of the time, sometimes amazed me with their understanding. One evening nine-year-old Misha suggested I read Psalm 40. She said she thought of me when she read it.

Psalm 40:1–2 says, 'I waited patiently for the Lord to help me, and he turned to me and heard my cry. He lifted me out of the pit of despair, out of the mud and the mire. He set my feet on solid ground and steadied me as I walked along.'

Verse 11–13 continues, 'Lord, don't hold back your tender mercies from me. My only hope is in your unfailing love and faithfulness. For troubles surround me – too many to count! They pile up so high I can't see my way out. They are more numerous than the hairs on my head. I have lost all my courage. Please, Lord, rescue me! Come quickly, Lord, and help me.'

And verse 17 states, 'As for me, I am poor and needy. But the Lord is thinking about me right now. You are my helper and my Saviour. Do not delay, O my God.'

I thought the author, King David and I were definitely on the same page, and I was awed by my eldest daughter's perceptiveness.

God I Don't Like You

Now that Mark was not terminally ill we began lots of extra doctor's visits, which were especially demanding because after long hours sitting in hospital waiting rooms, I still had all the routine tasks to keep four little girls fed, bathed, and looked after each evening. There was school homework to supervise, fresh clothes and school lunches to be prepared for the next day.

On a typical day when we'd endured an extremely long visit to a hospital optometrist who'd come to the rather obvious conclusion that Mark needed glasses, we'd arrived home overtired in the late afternoon still faced with all the normal afternoon chores.

By 6:30 p.m. I was officially losing the plot. Everywhere I turned something needed to be done and needed me to do it. The youngest two girls needed bathing; the oldest two needed pushing to have showers. The dishes needed to be cleaned and the washing needed sorting. Homework for four little girls needed supervising and of course Mark was asking for a drink and needed help getting to the lounge.

As I started yelling at them all in complete tiredness and frustration, I reflected that this was exactly what I was so mad about when the doctor told us the MRI results. What was once a dual effort was now a solo production, and the buck stopped with me.

As if the day wasn't already going badly enough, a lovely couple who had been financially assisting us each week chose to ring and tell us they were going to stop the weekly payments they'd been making to help us out. They had been so generous, and I was so incredibly thankful for their support, but I just couldn't believe the Lord was allowing another punch out of nowhere and this one was a biggie. We barely survived financially on what we had been receiving and now we would have to manage on $100 a week less.

I collapsed on the floor after the phone call. I felt I just could not take another knock down. Misha came over to me, gave me a hug and said, 'God will take care of us Mum, it says in the Bible not to worry.'

Thank you Lord, you truly do speak through the mouths of babes. In the Bible, Job went through a multitude of hardships and he still said, 'though he (God) slay me, yet will I trust him'. I felt with Job on that one.

I was trying to put a brave face on everything; 'Yes that's fine that you are not going to bring us any more meals, I understand. . . Thank you so much for the money you've given us, we will be fine without it.' But inside I was not coping at all. I was breaking apart.

At the first neurology appointment after Mark's necrosis diagnosis, Dr. Anderson explained again the unlikelihood of anyone suffering this awful side effect. But Mark had suffered it. This was just a very rare, unlucky chance?

As a result of the meeting, the doctors set in place a plan to try and readjust Mark's medications, because he still suffered continual pain. They also swapped morphine for a less-sedating drug.

Mark remained dependent on others for almost every daily chore. The girls often had to help him put his shoes on and get his drinks and food for him. They were great with him and when he had his seizures they would rub his back.

To cope with it, the girls and I developed a wicked sense of humor about cancer, illness, seizures and even death. I was exhausted most of the time, sometimes to extreme limits. When I fell into bed at night, it took an earthquake to shake me awake. One night I thought I dreamed I heard a persistently annoying noise, like a very loud mosquito. I swatted at it to stop it, and the noise faded into the distance. It wasn't till the morning I discovered that the noise was six-year-old Jasmine crying.

She had woken in the night scared and had come to me for comfort. All she got was an 'out-of-it' Mum cuffing her away, so she went back to her own bed, still crying. I was exhausted in every way, and I was grumpy and short-tempered most of the time. Mark often wore the brunt of my anger and as often as I got mad at him, he always forgave me for my dreadful behavior.

He was reliant on me for everything. As so often happens in close relationships, even when he was being looked after by someone else, he waited for me to get home to do certain things, although he could have asked the person who was temporarily caring for him.

My journal records clearly chronicle how I was feeling: 15 August 2003; 'I am embarrassed to say it, but Mark's illness is like this burden tied around my neck, dragging me down. I'm in the water and I'm slowly been pulled to the bottom and I'm drowning in it. There is no way to be pulled back to the surface and this is where everything is going to die.

'My dreams, passions, desires, freedom, hope, and my strength — all drowning. Yesterday I came to the conclusion that I felt hopeless. Not for eternity, not for Mark or the girls, but for me. Me personally – everything I had hoped and desired has to be flushed away and I feel hopeless. I have nothing except God.

'I know all His promises and that is what I cling to. His promises in his word. But not for me personally. That is where I am. I have been given this vision that I will touch and speak to an endless sea of people, but now I am in the valley.'

Reprimanded By Others

My struggle to cope did not go unnoticed by others who took it upon themselves to voice their disapproval of my conduct. As if my own self condemnation wasn't enough to handle, a knock down came from two people who I thought really had more of a clue. They arrived at my front door within minutes of each other, although apparently they had not planned it that way, and gave it to me with both barrels.

They informed me I sounded angry towards Mark, and I obviously needed a break (although apparently they were not offering to give me one). They told me I was constantly horrible to Mark. That I had talked about nothing but the radiation scarring. They felt so sorry for poor Mark because I was so horrible and angry.

They cited particular instances that had offended their sensibilities. It felt to me like they carried on and on. And far from shamed and submissive, I retaliated, yelling back, telling them they had no idea. When they left, I was a mess.

I couldn't believe they could be so lacking in empathy. Rather than feeling deferential, my reaction was 'How dare they?' They had not been given a life sentence of looking after a very sick man. They had not just been told that there was nothing the doctors could do and their husband would never get well. I was so hurt and angry. I could not believe that they could so easily cast stones when they had never had to live through anything like it themselves.

I was fully aware that I was not coping. I was drowning and angry, and I hated that I was taking my anger out on Mark. But I had no idea how to process this for all of us, not just for me, but for Mark, who was the one who was sick, and for our young daughters. I felt lower than low.

I was obviously doing the worst job of showing Jesus in my pain. In my journal I cried out: 'I confess it! I don't know how to come to terms with the radiation necrosis that has caused permanent brain damage in the most wonderful of men – my husband. I don't know what to do...HELP JESUS!'

Documentary View

There were a few key events that buoyed us up. When the documentary that Rob Harley and Lisa Walker made aired on *Inside New Zealand*, it evoked an amazing response. Titled *A Matter of Life and Death – the Mark Holmes Story*, it gave us joy and encouragement to know that God was still using us to reach people and be a witness for Him. People who knew us said that we had made them very proud. We had people contacting us from all over New Zealand. Typical of the response were letters like this:

'Dear Suzie, Mark and girls,

Thank you so much for your courage and convictions. How wonderful to hear from your daughter about Daddy going to Jesus. Children accept things so readily and believe so easily. You are all fantastic witnesses and I'm sure your rewards will be worth all the pain.

My husband went to glory nearly two years ago after a battle with cancer. Going through that, we found we both had a lot to thank God for. I just wanted you both to know what a fabulous witness you all are and I'm certain there are a lot of people left 'wondering' after your program.'

'Dear Suzanne,

It was with sorrow, joy and pride that I watched your family documentary. Thank you for sharing it with the nation. As someone who has cared for a loving husband with brain cancer for nine years I know what it feels like when you feel you yourself have ceased to exist......It is courage that is needed when a crisis has ceased to be exciting and has become instead a new version of your life to which you must now adjust.'

'Dear Susie and Mark,

My heart was indeed touched last evening as I watched you both and the children on TV. I thank you for your honesty and reality as you 'told it as it is'. I felt so much for you in your difficult situation. But, oh how I did rejoice in your closing statement, 'One day this will all turn out right – something really good.'

The ironic thing is if the documentary crew had continued filming for a few months longer than they did, they would have seen a very different Suzanne, although the cracks were already beginning to show.

God You Are Mean

Those high points were few and far between in a wasteland of lost hopes, debilitating pain and anguish. For all my high-minded desire to walk by faith, I just couldn't help starting to feel, 'God is mean.'

When Mark had a particularly bad week I returned to my feeling that I 'just wanted it over' — over for him, for me and for the girls. His impairment lingered like some bad smell that wouldn't go away. I railed at God, and accused him of not caring. I asked, 'Why us God? Why does Mark have to go through this?

'It's not death, it's worse. It's the complete loss of dignity, of personality, of independence and of him. Death would be a release and instead he faces this living nightmare. Why him? He loved and loves you. He served you with his life. You were first. Why him?

'And why this disgusting, slow, cruel life to death? Why do you allow it to stretch out? Why do you allow the nausea and vomiting? Why have you allowed the loss of speech? Why do you allow him to have no dignity? He's thirty-four! Not an old man.

'Why, why have you done this – prolonged this? It is just mean now. That is all it is. If you loved him and us as much as we think you do, why do you allow this to go on and on and on and on and on? There is no end! My cool, talented husband has suffered TOO MUCH! TOO MUCH! DO YOU HEAR GOD? He does not deserve this!'

Most upsetting of all, our oldest daughter Misha, the one who has been closest to Mark and seen the most of him, now began to mock him; she no longer expressed the respect she once had for him. I tried to understand that she did not know how to express her hurt that her Dad is not the Father he was, he is no longer well so she takes it out on him. I can hardly criticize, for I have become hard and callous myself.

'I am at a loss to explain how I can be totally devoted to Almighty God on the one hand, but at the same time cannot shake this conviction that God is mean. How can my heart love and adore my Saviour and yet be breaking completely? And yet this is what I am battling.

'I am asking why – knowing full well I will never get the answer, knowing full well that this prayer changes nothing, knowing full well these tears mean nothing. It is all in your hands God. I would like to say I can't do this anymore, but I know I will.

'The only thing I cling to is the hope that you will do something amazing through us. That is my life line. I know it is not for me to know why, but I do ask. Why Mark? He was such a great husband and Dad. He loves you Jesus. Why do you do this? Please release him into your hands before he loses anymore dignity. He does not deserve anymore. He never moans or complains. Please Father, have mercy!'

CHAPTER ELEVEN
HOME BECOMES A SICK WARD

'Patience is not the ability to wait, but the ability to keep a good attitude while waiting.' - Joyce Meyer, *Battlefield of the Mind: Winning the Battle in Your Mind.*

PEOPLE ARE always surprised that our home has lots of pretty 'decorator touches' when we've always lived on a very modest budget. How we achieved this comes down to genetics and determination. I was fussy from birth, the kind of two-year-old who liked to clean her room and wanted everything to look perfect. If a picture on the wall is out of alignment, I notice and can't refrain from straightening it.

I guess when Mark got ill the one area of our lives that I felt I could control was our surroundings. Whatever the reason, our new grim reality sparked in me a passion for home decorating that had previously lain dormant. Stripping paint and making plans to recover an armchair was a great distraction from the tough stuff going on daily, and helped me feel I could at least create beauty somewhere.

I watched TV home shows avidly and became an enthusiastic adherent to a 'shabby chic, country house, do-it-yourself' decorating style epitomized by interior designers like the UK's

Cath Kidson and Canadian Sarah Richardson. I taught myself to sew, tile, do mosaics, and strip old paint.

I spent hours searching out second hand bargain-price couches and side tables that I then transformed with sandpaper, paint and fabric. I collected Kidson's quirky floral homeware — friends always knew a Kidson mug would be a welcome birthday gift — and I made flowery cushions and learned how to do patchwork.

Whenever we got another bad medical report, I redecorated another room. People would come to visit and Jasmine and Emerald would be sleeping in the lounge because I was painting their bedroom. When Mark got his radiation necrosis diagnosis I redecorated the lounge. My home — and particularly my bedroom — was my sanctuary. And so when I had to start accommodating all the paraphernalia that accompanied permanent disability, it was another wrench.

First, as Mark began to use his walker less and needed his wheelchair more frequently, Neil and I had to rearrange my bedroom furniture so the chair could be wheeled straight into the room. My bedroom no longer looked like the lovely sanctuary room I had so lovingly created. It looked messy and over-crowded. I was so mad that cancer dominated every damn thing. Nearly every room in the house demonstrated how illness was altering my family's life.

The lounge furniture had to be organized entirely around the demands of getting the wheelchair freely in and out. The hall had to be set up so there was a clear wheelchair run from the lounge to the bedroom. Then a massive hoist arrived; another giant reminder of our situation, to be used as an aid when Mark fell. I admit, I resented the hoist so much I banished it to the garage and the girls and I managed to move Mark from his wheelchair to the bed without it.

Other changes were more welcome. The daily shower had become too much for me to manage. I was pleased and relieved when Mark accepted a proposal early in 2004 for a daily helper to come in to help shower him. Before the daily helper came, the shower took two and a half hours every morning.

And finally I was signing for the alterations to the bathroom so it could be made into a wheelchair accessible bathroom for Mark. The Ministry of Health (part of the New Zealand Government) was paying for all of this, which was a huge blessing. But there was the proof that illness consumed my life. I was no longer just Suz with a calling to serve God; I was a home help, nurse and caregiver. It was all bloody consuming and I hated it!

CHAPTER TWELVE
RUNNING AWAY FROM HOME

"'What makes the desert beautiful," said the little prince, "is that somewhere it hides a well.'" - Antoine de Saint-Exupéry, *The Little Prince*.

FOR MY THIRTY-THIRD birthday my friend Belinda had commissioned a painting of the desert that I still adore and which hangs on our lounge room wall even now. To me the image of a desert is a wonderful place - a place of refuge, and of peace.

Often I'd been drawn to Hosea 2:14–15 which says, 'I will lead her out to the desert and speak tenderly to her there. I will return her vineyards to her and transform the valley of trouble into a gateway of hope. She will give herself to me there.' The sense I got from Hosea was that even though the desert was a harsh place, there was still life and growth there. Even in this arid place God was going to make Himself real to me.

But it was also somewhere place to escape, and I began to entertain thoughts of running away, and even started planning how to do it. I began to understand I didn't want to run away from Mark; I just wanted to run away from this illness. Once not so long ago, before Mark got ill, I had tried to live a life as an upright Christian woman. Now I was humbled to discover what I feared most. And that was: I may have no moral guard left.

I was so lacking in feelings of warmth and affection in my marriage that I was worried if the right man — any man for that matter — came along and showed me the slightest bit of attention I might have succumbed and done what I feared the most. Have an affair.

I realized all over again that before this illness I would have been disapproving and judgmental of someone who left their spouse because of prolonged illness. How naïve was I? I was overwhelmed with a new awareness. Until we've walked a mile or two in someone's shoes we have no right to pass judgment. At least I was learning something from all this, I think.

I pleaded with Jesus to keep me from being unfaithful; I begged Him to be my protection and strength and keep me completely safe from that possibility. And I felt led to read Ezekiel 36:9, 'See, I am concerned for you and I will come to help you. Your ground will be tilled and your crops planted.'

Verse 26 continues, 'And I will give you a new heart with new and right desires and I will put a new spirit in you. I will take out your stony heart of sin and give you a new obedient heart and I will put my spirit in you so you will obey my laws and do whatever I command. . . I will cleanse you of your filthy behavior. I will give you good crops and I will abolish famine in the land (29).

Verse 36–37 notes, 'Then the nations all around – all those still left – will know that I the Lord rebuilt ruins and planted lush crops in the wilderness. For I the Lord have promised this and I will do it. This is what the sovereign Lord says: I am ready to hear Israel's prayers for these blessings and I am ready to grant their requests.'

As I was emptied out of my self-righteousness, as I lost my natural strength, I was left feeling empty. This was not a bad thing though. I was starting to comprehend that although I loved the Lord with all my heart, there was still tons more of me in my life than there was of Him. I asked Belinda if it was okay for me to leave Mark. But no, there is no out in the Bible for this, actually the vows we made were 'in sickness and in health.'

But I did feel stuck in a ridiculous marriage and stuck looking after Mark. No matter how much you love someone, four years of this would test anyone's commitment, wouldn't it? But I did desire to finish this well. I just honestly sometimes felt like I would fail. Jesus had to step in and do something. The longer the illness went on and the sicker Mark got, the more I saw all my bad points. They stood out bold and bright. I needed all of God's help just to be nice to Mark. Isn't that terrible? He needed so much help, and I didn't want to do any of it, but was obligated to do it.

Psalm 55:6–7 says, 'Oh how I wish I had wings like a dove, then I would fly away and rest! I would fly far away to the quiet of the wilderness.' This was what I often thought; just let me run away. Let this hideous situation be not mine anymore.

And the same Psalm, verse 16–17 adds, 'But I will call on God and the Lord will rescue me. Morning, noon and night I plead aloud in my distress and the Lord hears my voice.' I was sure the Lord heard my voice. Selfishness really did rule more of my life than I would have liked to admit.

I was realizing this time of ruin was a good thing because it was also a time of cleansing. It had only come after I had to confess for months that I did completely surrender. I didn't like 'the me I saw' anyway. I was more than happy for Jesus to get rid of that person. Naturally and bizarrely we cling to what we are. Desiring to hold onto that 'me' seems increasingly ridiculous.

Great Escape

A year after the radiation necrosis diagnosis, the girls and I managed to get away for a week with Belinda and her boys while Mark was cared for in a respite facility. We stayed at Belinda's aunt and uncle Waikato's farmhouse while they were away on holiday, and it was bliss.

I didn't get up until 10:00 a.m. and then we sat outside on an old couch sipping coffee and overlooking the most beautiful peaceful farmland view. I didn't have to cut up anyone's food. I was with people whose legs and arms worked. There was no one saying, 'I'm going to throw up.' The heaviness and burden of Mark's everyday life was absent.

But my week of freedom just made it all the harder to return to my prison with a good attitude. After being back home for two days, I felt like I was breaking apart. I had had a vague glimpse of what life could be like without radiation necrosis, and the reality was harder to accept than ever. I wandered around the house doing the chores, but inside, my emotions were a churning volcano. I headed out to the garage where our washing machine was located to do the wash and I took a long hard look at the handily parked car.

Suddenly, the way out was blindingly obvious. All I had to do was put the girls in the car, get in and drive away. It was as simple as that. Just a couple of actions and I could leave, I could be free of radiation necrosis. I started sobbing and crying out to the God who had left me. I screamed as loud as I could at God as I stood by the car; 'I'm going God, do you hear, I am going and I know I will suck in the sight of many people, but no one else has to live this shit, just me, and I have had enough. I'm not doing this anymore, I am leaving.'

In my head I didn't know if I was going permanently or temporarily, I was just gripped by the idea, and I no longer cared what the world or God thought anymore. Then one of the girls brought the phone out to me. Trying to pull myself together I answered, 'Hello?' A woman's voice said; 'You probably don't remember me, I'm a friend of Carolyn's and I have just rung Carolyn to get your phone number because you are on my mind, are you alright?'

She was right; I didn't remember her, but talk about stunned, how did she know I was not alright? I couldn't have said I was fine even if I wanted to, so I answered very honestly, 'No, I'm shit! I can't do this, any of this, anymore.'

For over half an hour I sobbed on the phone to her, letting all my frustration, anger and grief come to the surface. This poor woman heard it all, my thoughts and my feelings. I wasn't holding anything back. And she just kept saying, 'You are going to make it through this, you are going to make it through this.'

When she finally hung up, I quietly cried, 'God, I'm not an idiot, I know that was you. You got her to ring me right when I was preparing to leave, you got her to listen to all my mess and you got her to encourage me that I can do this and I will. You have not left me, you are here, you have been silent for so long but you have not forgotten me. Thank you for rescuing me today, thank you for telling her to ring, thank you for not giving up on me, thank you for not letting me leave and making a massive mistake that I know I will regret. Thank you for it all!'

Only God knew I was on the point of leaving, only God knew that I needed to hear from someone completely outside of the know, only God could have put me on her mind that she had to ring to see if I was okay. She was God's mouthpiece that day; God used her to reach me in a way only God could. God had saved me from making a big mistake and He showed me He hadn't left me. For the first time in ages I could feel the God who comforts!

The next three days the phone rang constantly from friends all over the country asking 'are you alright, I can't stop thinking and praying for you.' God was showing me how much He truly cared for me by placing me on the hearts of people all over New Zealand. I got to the bottom and what I landed on was a solid rock and that rock was God. Thank you for being there when I reached the end.

Thank you for not deserting me when I needed you most and being there in the depth of my darkness. What I noticed was that the more I tried to run away from God, the more I was running in a circle straight toward Him. Not that I was trying to forget Him or anything, but I was trying to forget His will.

Now I was back begging God to do something because only He could. The other thing I managed to articulate while chatting to Belinda was this – I'm too young for this to be my life sentence. I don't know if I had ever put it in those words before.

At thirty-four I was too young for this to be the end of marriage and all the benefits that went with it. Mark was too young to be dealing with a chronic and possibly terminal illness. We are too young! My heart, in desperation, turned more to God than ever. In my attempt to tell God to flag it and that I was leaving and didn't care about the consequences, I actually ended up back with Him, pleading for Him to fix it all.

CHAPTER THIRTEEN
THE PASTOR'S WIFE HAS WISDOM

'Never, ever determine the truth of a situation by looking at the circumstances.' - *Experiencing God,* Henry T. Blackaby & Claude V. King.

I WAS FEELING desperate for God, but when the pastor's wife, Theresa started pestering me about taking part in a weekly women's Bible study on the topic of *Experiencing God* I privately decided she's a real pain in the butt.

I can only think that the truth of our situation was a little hidden from me. To look beyond the circumstances was going to take a divine revelation from God who of course can see the end from the beginning, and fully understands the reason for this illness. I was experiencing a roller coaster ride of emotions every day, but, at this point, I was no longer so mad at God; the anger had been replaced by sadness and numbness.

But the last thing on this entire earth that I wanted to do was a Bible study with a whole bunch of women who have no idea what I am going through and whose biggest problem was their naughty kids. I thought I had engineered my way out when I discovered the study was planned for Tuesday mornings — the day I taught four swimming classes, so I could tell her 'bummer I can't make it.'

She came back asking, 'When are you free?' Because I really didn't want to do the study, I made it as hard as I could for her and said I was only free on Fridays at lunchtime. And for goodness sake she had come back with, 'Okay, Friday lunchtime it is, just you and me.' That wasn't what I saw happening and I was quite dumbfounded that I was part of this Bible study. God was obviously determined it was going to take place.

But even if I couldn't stand the idea of doing a study on *Experiencing God,* I was also absolutely desperate for God. For all that He is and can supposedly do; I feel sick with nerves because I grasped how close to the edge I was, so close to the edge that I nearly left Mark. I couldn't believe how low I had fallen.

'Jesus, I'm desperate for you. You haven't forgotten me, you have shown that, but that hasn't changed anything about my situation. Life is still shit, and I really need you to help me cope with today,' I said.

July 23, 2004: Despite my reluctance, the first study was a revelation. It led me to put into words something I didn't realize until now; 'I am scared of what God's will for my life may be.' My fear stemmed from the anxiety that His will was for Mark to live on as he is or just slowly deteriorate further for years and years, both of us trapped.

I felt that even two or three years would be more than I could take. It's not that I was tempted to just strike out, forgetting about God and doing my own thing, because I actually thought I would mess my life up even more if I attempted that, but I was simply terrified of what the future held.

The Bible study encouraged us to pray, 'Where are you at work, God?' and wait to see what He was up to. So that was what I was praying, 'Where are you at work in my family and my life?' The Bible says in 2 Samuel 22:31, 'As for God, his way is perfect.' Which means that this debilitating disease and all that comes with it is perfect? How? No idea! But apparently I could trust Him.

My prayer became, 'Soften my heart, God.' Because I am also understanding that I am hardening my heart to God. Hard people are angry and bitter. It's our defense and our wall. If I'm angry I can't hope, and then when good things don't happen I won't get hurt. But I don't want to be bitter. I want to be soft. I guess being soft opens me up to being hurt.

I know that in the emptiness, I felt work going on. It's like a gardener with a hoe turning the soil (soul) and getting rid of the weeds. After weeding and clearing out old plants, which in my case are wrong thoughts, desires, selfishness, pride, and jealousy, there comes the dressing of the compost and the fertilizer which is Jesus, His word and the Holy Spirit. God's fertilizer is good. It is all good and it is going to be great!

As Lamentations 3:20–33 says, 'I will not forget this awful time as I grieve over my loss. Yet I still dare to hope when I remember this' (20–21). 'The unfailing love of the Lord never ends! By his mercies we have been kept from complete destruction. Great is his faithfulness, his mercies begin afresh each day. I say to myself "the Lord is my inheritance, therefore I will hope in him!"' (22–24).

'The Lord is wonderfully good to those who wait for him and seek him. So it is good to wait quietly for salvation from the Lord and it is good for the young to submit to the yoke of his discipline' (25–27). 'Though he brings grief, he also shows compassion according to the greatness of his unfailing love. For he does not enjoy hurting people or causing them sorrow.' (32–33).

In all of history there has always been loss, grief, hard times and sadness. Some is caused by the consequence of our own wrongdoing, some by the consequences of others and some is just allowed. I know ours has been allowed. It is here and permeating all parts of our lives.

I do grieve the loss of my loving and very cool husband, the father of my children, my best friend, but also I grieve over my loss of freedom as this illness has trapped me. But Jeremiah says here 'I STILL DARE TO HOPE… ' and that is me. I still dare to hope that because of the Lord's unfailing love, He will bring something great out of all this.

July 28 2004: I have woken up feeling broken. I don't know what the switch was, but something has happened inside me. I cannot describe the sadness that is overwhelming me. I look at my girls, comprehending how desperately I love them. I feel like a little girl, lost, unloved and lonely. I choose God today! I am reminding myself all day that God's way is perfect! I may feel sad but I cannot and will not let emotions dictate my day. I have been working on my *Experiencing God* Bible study which was really interesting last night.

It said God gives you the assignment – then works on your character until you are ready to fulfill that assignment. Character building can take years. Apparently it was twenty-five years from Abraham's call that he would be the father of a nation to the time Isaac was born. Obviously this is my character building time. This is really encouraging. Deuteronomy 32:4 says, 'His works are perfect.'

In my study today it asked, 'Do I love God with all my heart?' I realize I do and that I want to be His little girl. In this study it says everything depends on the quality of our love relationship with God. If it is not right then nothing will be right. I guess that is part of the reason I have been so angry at God.

I love Him with everything in me and He loves me as His precious daughter. I know that being a parent you want the best for your children because you love and adore them. I would not have allowed what God has allowed in Mark's and my life to my worst enemy and yet the God who loves me has allowed it.

But this is what I am really learning; I do not understand Him or His ways at all. That is what makes Him God! His ways are perfect but they are out of our realm of understanding. This is the same lesson my soul mate Job learned 4000 years ago and I am only just starting to grasp now. God is odd!

In the *Experiencing* Bible study this week we were asked to really look at God's love for us. His love that is real, personal and practical. As I thought over my life and all it involved, I had to say I did love God and I had to acknowledge that He did love me. There is too much evidence leading me to this conclusion and too much of my life is wrapped up in Him. Why does He keep this going? Why does He allow Mark to be like this? Why does He allow me to live this crap? I don't know, yet I cannot say He doesn't love me because I see His love in lots of other things.

I see it in the way He takes care of the little things for my girls. I see it in how He allows them to continue to excel in their lives even though they are living in these tough circumstances. And I see it in the kindness, in the anonymous gifts that come to us at crucial times, bailing us out of financial holes.

August 13, 2004: At the Bible study today I told Theresa that I found this week's study hard because I wasn't impressed where obedience to God's will had gotten me. Mark and I have always been, to the best of our ability, obedient to God's plan for our lives, so I am having trouble processing that it is still the best way to do life.

CHAPTER FOURTEEN
GETTING BACK ON MY FEET

'The most powerful idea that's entered the world in the last few thousand years - the idea of grace - is the reason I would like to be a Christian.' - Bono, U2.

AS I WORK my way through this *Experiencing God* study, it challenges what I have let myself believe since Mark's diagnosis of necrosis. It is actually reaffirming the faith I used to have in God that has been so badly shaken over the last year.

I am starting to see that since I began desperately seeking God a few months ago my attitude has changed. I see much more good in each day, and I am sensing God is more present in my day.

Our *Experiencing God* Scripture for the week's study was Hebrews 11:6, 'Without faith it's impossible to please God. He who loves God must believe he exists and he rewards those who earnestly seek him.'

And I wonder if maybe the reward that is talked about in this verse isn't a change in my circumstance, but rather a change of my attitude in my circumstance. I realized there were areas of my life that were not what I wanted, but there were many areas of my life that were truly blessed, like my beautiful healthy four daughters, my amazing family and friends, the lovely home the Lord had given us to live in and of course the blessed land, New Zealand, that I get to call home.

When Misha's eleventh birthday rolls around in late August we indulge in one of our long-standing family traditions – the birthday date with Mum - and I am reminded all over again that in the midst of our hardship we still share special times. These birthday dates are my four favourite days of the year. We spend the day having lunch together and shopping for new clothes for the 'birthday girl.' My day out with Misha this year was no exception. It was so much fun watching her choose clothes and listening to her chat about school and friends with no competition from her three sisters.

In my Bible study we've been considering the question of how truth and fact are different. Fact: In the gospels the disciples were in a boat, in a bad storm and they were going to drown (Matthew 8, Mark 4, Luke 8). Truth: Jesus, the truth, was in the boat and when He spoke the storm went completely still.

Fact: David was quite small compared with the giant Goliath (1 Samuel 17). Truth: David went to kill Goliath in the name of the Lord and with faith that God would use him to destroy the giant. And he did. Fact: We have never had any money to ever travel overseas. Truth: We have lived in many different countries through God's miraculous provision.

Fact: Our Government Invalid's benefit isn't enough to cover all of our needs. Truth: Financially, God provides all the time and we have enough. Fact: My life sucks and I don't like the situation I am in. Truth: Jesus says we have hope in Him and through Him.

I am praying so hard for faith to believe that the future is going to be good. Not for the future to be good, but to have the faith to believe it will be. My faith has been so shaken in the things of God. Not God Himself, but in my understanding of Him and His ways.

As September rolls on I have been focusing my prayers and thoughts on what Paul wrote in Philippians 4:11, 'I have learned to be content in any and every situation. Whether well fed or hungry, whether living in plenty or in want' (NIV).

The Apostle Paul was in a Roman prison when he wrote that. Through his years of ministry he had learned contentment in all situations and there he was in prison writing for the believers in Philippi, telling then that despite his imprisonment he was content.

I wanted that kind of contentment. My situation was nothing like Paul's, in fact I think he would tell me to pull my head in. And yet discontent ruled my thoughts and made me unsatisfied with all that was around me.

It bred in me attitudes like jealousy of others who have healthy husbands who earn good money, a lack of joy because I was so dissatisfied with my lot, a total lack of patience at the man I love, a quick and bad temper at Mark and the girls, and also I could moan a lot out loud so others heard my discontentment.

All these horrible habits made life harder than it needed to be. I must learn to be content in all areas. I regularly prayed that scripture and said it out loud every time I thought a thought that I know would lead to discontentment. I wanted to say as Paul did two thousand years ago, 'I have learned to be content in any and every situation.'

25 September 2004: I knew I had to read Ezra 3 and I also knew I had to look at the whole story about the rebuilding of the temple in Jerusalem after it had been destroyed by the Babylonians. These verses really stood out. Ezra 3:10–13:

'When the builders completed the foundation of the Lord's temple, the priests put on their robes and took their places to blow their trumpets. And the Levites, the descendants of prominent temple leader Asaph, clashed their cymbals to praise the Lord, just as King David had prescribed, with praise and thanks they sang this song to the Lord. "He is so good! His faithful love for Israel endures forever."

'Then all the people gave a great shout, praising the Lord because the foundation of the Lord's Temple had been laid. Many of the older priests, Levites and other leaders remembered the first Temple and they wept aloud when they saw the new Temple's foundation. The others however were shouting for joy. The joyful shouting and weeping mingled together in loud commotion that could be heard far in the distance.'

Could God be saying He has finished my new foundation? After He seems to have smashed all my thinking patterns, my thoughts, my attitudes, and my relationship with Him over the last four years and especially this year — has my base been rebuilt? Is it time to praise God for that? I think this is what God is saying. One minute I am excited, the next I have never felt more like I an empty shell. I feel I have less to give than I've ever had. And yet this is probably the exact place God wants me to be because my foundation, the core of who I am, has to be less of me and more of Him.

Maybe this is what Paul means in Galatians 2:20 when he speaks of dying to self. 'It is no longer I that live but Christ that lives in me.' I must die to self and live to Christ. My main concern and motivator is no longer made up of my ideas, my way of interpreting God's word and His ways, my concept of life. That core is now firmly based on God being the Almighty Creator of the Universe. God who knows the End from the

Beginning. God who is all powerful, is everywhere and at the same time all loving. The God whose ways are so different from mine.

As Isaiah 55:8–9 says, 'My thoughts are completely different from yours, says the Lord. And my ways are far beyond anything you could imagine. For just as the heavens are higher than the earth, so my ways are higher than your ways and my thoughts higher than your thoughts.'

That is the new foundation I am now starting with. And like the older priests in Ezra there has been weeping at the work it has taken to get here, but I choose to celebrate like the others with shouts of joy at the work God has done in me.

Late September 2004: I am having more good days than bad ones. I can say this is a miracle. I'm sure it's got something to do with being thankful for every little — and sometimes ridiculous — thing. As I near the end of 2004, I can see God in His gentleness has walked me out of the worst years of my life. I am still extremely tired all the time and I still have my very bad days. Unfortunately, my swearing can still be pretty foul and I still lose it often, but a change is slowly happening.

Years ago a friend had a vision of me when she was praying for me; I was a beautiful blue vase. She watched as the vase fell backward and smashed into a million pieces into two hands cupped beside each other and then slowly the hands started mending the vase and it became more beautiful than before. Well I have truly been smashed, and I do feel like I am very carefully being pieced back together.

The *Experiencing God* Bible study I have done with Theresa has been part of the glue. It has renewed my spirit and confirmed to me that I do hear God and that despite circumstances God is in control because I gave Him my life and control of it years before. But most of the glue has come from my early morning times spent with God, reading and believing His word.

Friends, family and even strangers have been wonderful with their encouragement in helping rebuild me, but nothing, and I mean nothing, can replace the time I have spent one on one with the Almighty God. That was the very reason He created us – so He could have fellowship with us.

As I take time each day to hear from Him, I am taking time to be healed by Him. He has led me to so many scriptures in the Bible that I never knew were there. He has led me to the perfect scripture for each day. No one else can do that.

One of His names is Jehovah Rapha – the God who heals. And some of the biggest wounds in our lives, human eyes never see. But I am a walking testimony that He is the God who heals the broken hearted. I still battle with things, but I no longer feel the despair I had six months ago. God says in Isaiah 61:3, He will give 'a crown of beauty instead of ashes, the oil of joy instead of mourning, and a garment of praise instead of a spirit of despair.' I feel that change.

I know I am nowhere near healed. I still feel a raw anger towards Mark for this illness. I know that is unfair, and yet to be honest, I know it is there. That is something God has to work on, since I cannot. But I take heart that these are the early days. It has been only a year and a half since the radiation necrosis diagnosis. That blew me off my feet spiritually and emotionally.

I am only just starting to get up now, and I am aware there is still a long way to go before I am standing; perhaps God knows being on my knees is best. But my confidence is in the promise Jesus left us in Mark 10:27, 'With men it is impossible, but not with God; for with God all things are possible.'

PART III-
CATTLE ON 1000 HILLS

'How Does God Provide?'

2000 – 2014

Chapter Fifteen
Nothing Apart From Me

'I have learned that faith means trusting in advance what will only make sense in reverse.' - Philip Yancey.

WE LIVE IN a beautiful four bedroom, double-lounge, two bathroom home with a tiny mortgage, situated down a lovely peaceful Right of Way. That we managed to buy it at all is a daily reminder we serve a God who blesses us beyond our wildest dreams if we let Him have full control. I love sitting on our fully covered deck on a rainy day as much as a sunny one. In winter, I get a lot of pleasure from setting a roaring fire in the wood burning stove that warms the entire house.

We found joy here with our singing and dancing girls, even in the midst of Mark's illness. Cancer did not have the last word in our home. On the tightest of budgets we lived an expansive life; our big kitchen a centre of laughter, craziness, and music, although Mark was never again able to play his beloved guitar after his surgery.

In the nearly twenty years Mark and I were married, there were just four months that Mark had a really well-paying job, working as a video editor for a short period immediately before he fell ill. For the last nine years of Mark's life we lived on an

Invalid's Benefit or Accident-related Government provisions because of his treatment-related disability; for most of the first two years of our marriage Mark was unemployed, and for the other nine years we were urban missionaries living on charitable donations and the generosity of church members, friends and family. We didn't win the lottery or inherit a fortune. So, people are curious; just how did we do it?

When I occasionally get invited to speak at women's breakfasts and similar gatherings, this is often the most frequently asked question: How did you manage financially? And it was the first anxiety I faced after learning that Mark was terminally ill. I had no idea how to process the information that the doctors believed his life was going to be cut short by a brain tumor; but the question of 'How are we going to feed our family of four little girls next week?' was immediate and pressing.

Mark had been working long hours as a freelance film/video editor before he was diagnosed with cancer, but as a contract worker he had no rights to sick pay, holiday pay or medical benefits. We hadn't been back from overseas long so the little we had in the way of savings had been used up in getting settled.

What we did have was years of experience in living out the practical realities of Matthew's gospel, 'Therefore I tell you, do not worry about your life, what you will eat or drink; or about your body, what you will wear . . . Look at the birds of the air; they do not sow or reap or store away in barns, and yet your heavenly Father feeds them. Are you not much more valuable than they?' (Matt 6:25–26).

The house we live in now isn't even our first miracle house, but our third. Our first was a gorgeous hundred-year-old, tiny three-bedroom railway cottage, with a little veranda and a white picket fence bought with my parents help within eleven months of getting back to New Zealand from the US. It had high ceilings and wooden floors, an old fashioned fire place and sash windows.

I loved it so much I think we would still be living in it today, but its old stairs and narrow hallways made it impossible as a place to live once we accepted Mark would need a wheelchair and a bathroom modified for a person with mobility difficulties.

We bought our weatherboard railway cottage with nil equity, through the wonderful generosity of my parents. That meant we in effect did not put a cent down as a deposit. Twenty percent of the purchase price was borrowed against my Mum and Dad's house, and the other eighty percent on our house, with my parents acting as guarantor.

Our mortgage broker had his work cut out for him, trying to make our income look enough to cover the mortgage one hundred percent. But by some miracle after spending a few months door-knocking for work, Mark had just landed a full time editing job with Flying Start Pictures, and our income supported the mortgage application.

The railway house cost $157,000; we prayed that God would have His way and if we were supposed to have our own home that He would make it happen. Sure enough the Lord was amazing and the bank lent us the funds to let us buy our first little house. My Mum made it a condition of their help that Mark took out income protection insurance for the amount of the mortgage payments. Mark's Mum insisted we take out life insurance.

Mark and I struggled with how we were going to afford these two extra payments every month, but both of us felt we had to honor our parent's request so we took out both policies – something we would never have done if we weren't respecting our parents' wishes — and which became a huge unexpected blessing when Mark's cancer was diagnosed. It was furnished through amazing provision from unexpected gifts and God even provided us with two cars. People gave us so much furniture.

My dearest friends Steve and Cathy Wedgwood, (we had become friends when we had worked together before Mark and I went to Amsterdam) had decided God was calling them to China to teach English and so they gave us their bed and washing machine. We had shipped all the girls' beds and toys from the States so they had everything they needed.

Truly, if you walked into our house you would never have known that we had been away on the mission field; God provided for everything. I started adding our own personal touches and it felt like we were settling down for the very first time.

We'd arrived home in July, 1998, and by the following May we were ensconced in our own home with Mark in full time work. Misha and Bonnie were happily immersed in school and pre-school respectively.

In September 1999, Mark turned thirty. I decided to throw a massive surprise birthday party for him. Over 130 guests came; we had a thousand balloons decorating the hall and my brother Adam's band played.

I wanted to show Mark publicly how very much I loved him and how very much he was loved by friends and family alike. It was an amazing night in honor of my fantastic husband, the loyal and fun friend he was, and the loving father and son.

A few months later, on December 9th 1999, Mark surprised me with a beautiful eternity ring, for our tenth wedding anniversary. It was the first time we had ever spent money on something 'frivolous' like a ring.

I learned later that he went into the jeweller's and asked for a 'maternity ring' which of course had the sales people in hysterics.

We capped off our first decade together with a lovely dinner out, just the two of us. Our marriage had gone from strength to strength. We honestly loved each other more every passing year, and I was so thankful to God for all that he had blessed us with.

As the year drew to its close, we felt as if our lives overflowed with blessing. Mark had started a new career he was enjoying immensely and we owned our own little piece of paradise. We had done what God had asked of us and given the girls security and stability, and it seemed to be working out right for all of us.

CHAPTER SIXTEEN
STARTING OUT

'The church was never meant to be a noun. And when it turns into a noun, it becomes a turn off. The church was meant to be a verb, an action verb.'
- **Mark Batterson, *All In*.**

GOING BACK TO the early years, First Presbyterian, our home church in Auckland with its 'family' congregation of 300, understood better than many what it meant to be a verb. When we married, though we had very little money between the two of us, we had a grand plan to work with Youth with a Mission (YWAM) the international mission where Mark's family was working when I met him.

We'd both had experience in believing God for money before we married. Mark had shared these lessons on the mission field with his parents, who became Christians when he was ten years old. We'd both absorbed the Christian approach to money which we understood as: Work Hard, Give Generously and Pray.

We followed these principles wholeheartedly. From our first days together we'd tithed (given ten percent of our income to the church) as well as supported a child through Tear Fund. Even at our 'brokest' we never wavered from these commitments.

Our temperamental differences were reflected in the way we handled money. Mark — with his laid back approach — was pretty terrible at managing his dollars; my obsessive, organized personality, plus time spent working in a bank, meant I was pretty good at budgeting. However, we both shared in the decisions and we insisted that both of us understood everything about our finances in case something happened to one of us.

Into Our Calling

Within two years, we'd managed to elicit an invitation to Amsterdam through Mark's music connections; our missionary calling was endorsed and supported at three levels by First Presbyterian. Everyone there was devoted to mission outreach and they were generous givers.

There was a whole wall displaying pictures and information about the missionary families and several younger people working with YWAM who the church already supported. But they didn't just send anyone out. Getting approval from all three levels of the church leadership was not at all to be taken for granted. You had to have shown dedication to missions for a number of years, and we had.

First, a mission's board, then the elders, and then the finance board granted support for our move to Amsterdam, while family members — Mark's parents, and two of my uncles who were in ministry — also sought help from their churches.

I have always been a cheerleader for winning people to Christ and I talked — you might say raved — about practically nothing else. I had such a 'Let's do this together' attitude that when we left for Amsterdam there were sixty people at the airport to see us off.

Once we were in Europe, we took our responsibilities to administer the funds we received very seriously, and one of my roles was to keep in touch with our supporters and let them know what we were doing and how their support of around $2000 a month was being used.

We wrote a regular newsletter and sent hundreds of individual Christmas cards thanking people for their assistance. On visits back to New Zealand we met up with our supporters individually. We got terrific backing from them and we worked very hard to keep them in touch and maintain their interest.

So when Mark became fixated on the idea of getting dreadlocks we agreed we could not use our benefactor gifts for these kinds of frivolous personal expenses. Mark wasn't just your normal bloke, and I wasn't the only one who thought he was different. When Mark's Mum, Val, first saw the heavily tattooed Korn singer Brian Welch on TV she rang us up madly excited to say; 'There's someone who's as weird as Mark on TV!'

Mark loved piercings and tattoos and dreads — and I wasn't very keen on dreads and tattoos, so when he got madly enthused about a guy's dreadlocks he'd seen and wanted the same thing, I told him, 'We can't use supporter's money for that!'

Dreads were unusual and tattoos not common amongst Christians in 1994 and it cost about $300 to get them professionally done which was practically all the money we had, so he worked a private job for several days with our dear friend Matthew Mark, who had a courier run, to pay for them. And we made sure everyone knew Mark had earned the money for this little indulgence himself.

Busted Buskers

We loved our YWAM work, but even with our generous missionary support base, the NZ dollar did not go far in Europe and there were no five star hotels, tourist trips or restaurant dinners on the itinerary. Even with careful management, we sometimes saw lean times.

When we tried to supplement our food budget by busking on a Copenhagen street at Christmas, Mark and our drummer Neil Leatherbarrow got arrested. We hadn't understood it was against the law to busk before 4:00 p.m. and the boys had set up with their guitar, bucket drum and ironing board ten minutes before 4:00 p.m.

Our third wedding anniversary was spent stranded at the Norwegian/Swedish border crossing, after we'd been refused entry into Norway because Mark had left our passports under the mattress back at our last hostel. We'd hoped to avoid a check because passport control in this area was random.

We'd taken the gamble in the hope we could then just get our passports sent on to us, but we hadn't taken into account that a derelict red van, filled with young people towing a trailer with a stage coffin on it, was bound to attract attention. After three hours at a truck stop in 1 C temperatures unsuccessfully trying to hitch a ride back to collect our passports, I lost all warm fuzzy thoughts of how wonderful our first three years together had been and screamed at Mark for over an hour letting him know, in no uncertain terms, how dumb it was to be spending our wedding anniversary standing frozen on the side of the road.

Then God took over and truly rescued us. Our YWAM contacts organized a bed for the night with two former drug addicts who'd recently become Christians and lived in a little house not far from the border. This amazing couple couldn't speak English, but arranged to pick us up, and then they sat us in front of a roaring fire and fed us delicious Danish bread.

We were unaware they had prayed when they had moved into this house that God would bring anyone He wanted to stay because they wanted to bless and help His people… and the first people He brought were from the other side of the world.

In the morning, they took us down to the train station, paid for our trip to Stockholm and sent us off with a delicious packed lunch. To us, it was total luxury and an incredible example of God being in control no matter where we were in the world.

At the end of our band tour we discovered I was pregnant with our first child, and that set a pattern for the next few years of alternating our missions work and family life between New Zealand and the US. We delivered daughters number one and two in NZ, where we organized tours for YWAM bands and then moved on to a new missions 'start-up' in the US, punctuated by two European tours.

Mission X and Washington DC

Based out of Houston, Texas, we worked with Tim Bisagno and the First Baptist Church launching Mission X, aimed at reaching Post Baby Boomers through media, music and a relevant presentation of the gospel. We considered ourselves missionaries first and foremost: the music was simply a tool for God to use through us.

In April 1996, just before a tour to Poland and Germany, Mark's band The Friendlys was asked to play at a big 'Washington for Jesus' rally when President Bill Clinton was in office. It was the most amazing experience. The stage was set up in front of the Capitol Building in Washington DC, attracting an estimated 600,000 crowd which went wild all night. As a relatively unknown band, we got the 4:00 a.m. slot. Misha and Bonnie were two and a half years and fifteen months old at the time. They snuggled down in their sleeping bags with everyone else in front of the Capitol Building and slept through all the noise.

Back in Houston after the European tour, and a trip back to New Zealand for the birth of our third daughter Jasmine, we moved into the cutest little home — one of those old houses that had a massive veranda at the front with a swing seat in a great neighborhood — and our lives were everything we could have imagined.

We belonged to a fabulous church, Houston Vineyard, which we loved. They were supportive of Mission X and of us as a family and to add to the blessings, we had just found out we had a surprise coming in November, baby number four.

Mark and I decided that as it looked like we were staying in the US, I would start home schooling Misha. We sorted out a routine to allow for family life as well as our missionary focus. Mission X TV or MXTV's passion was - and is – to ensure that the 'Media Generation' encounters God. Continuously broadcasting for the last seventeen years, it prides itself on being the original voice in evangelistic multi-media for young people. Translated into six languages – with Arabic soon to be added – it offers an eclectic menu of alternative music, extreme sports, and relevant teaching that has aired on practically every Christian channel in the US as well as faith networks across 200 countries with a potential audience of 3.4 billion.

We were there at its inception, and some historic footage of Mark performing is still available (see Publishers Notes for details of weblinks.) With Mark learning how to edit on the job and Tim pulling it all together, they made it work with little experience and even smaller financial investment. Mark loved his new role, but was still very much committed to the band side of Mission X.

With everything that was happening around us; helping in building a new team, and recruiting new staff for the TV operation, we still made time as a family. We did the housework together after the girls were asleep. Mark never minded helping, and we considered our marriage a partnership where partners do an equal share of the work.

And even though MXTV was taking off, and the band was busy preparing for a tour to Spain, Germany and Austria, Mark still made an effort to be there for dinner and the girls' bedtime. His days consisted of band practice during the day and editing for MXTV in the evening, but without fail he was home for dinner and always helped put the girls to bed. He wanted to make sure his children never thought that ministry came before them.

Mark had been part of missionary circles since he was thirteen and so often he had seen families fall apart or teenagers make bad decisions because the family was put in second place to the mission. He was determined his girls would know his family was his first priority.

Life was an amazing adventure that Mark and I were journeying together. We saw the world as full of possibilities, and we were going to make sure we experienced as many of them as we could. And then as certainly as we had felt we were on a firm foundation, we felt our world turn to quicksand.

The New Zealand dollar took a big dive; eighty cents became fifty cents, which seriously undermined our financial support from home. We were renting our house from our church and although they halved our rent so we could afford to stay, we were feeling very unsettled.

With baby number four on the way, we acknowledged we had always preferred the free medical services in NZ compared with the health expenses we faced in the US. And although it went against what we wanted to do for ourselves, we both kept getting the sense that stability and security for our growing family needed to be our priority now.

Then Mark had a dream that we felt was from God. It was of the band being removed from Mission X and Mission X being more focused on MXTV. As the TV side of Mission X grew and the music side dwindled, Mark felt his role in Mission X was coming to an end.

By mid 1998, we knew for certain God was calling us back to New Zealand for a season. We were to give the girls security and stability, but at the same time we thought God would still use us on short term mission trips. We had grand plans of raising up musicians from New Zealand, training them up to do what we had done and then taking them to do it.

As far as we were concerned, we had not stopped, just slowed down and changed location. Mark brought the girls and me back to the little town where we had courted and married nine years earlier and then he headed off to Europe to do the last tour with The Friendlys, in Germany and Spain.

It wasn't what we wanted to do and obedience came at a huge price, but in hindsight it was a wonderful thing for us. God enabled us to get a home of our own and be settled amongst family before Mark's illness became apparent.

CHAPTER SEVENTEEN
LOOKING TO GOD

'God isn't concerned with your comfort, but with your character.' -Rick Warren, *The Purpose Driven Life*.

AFTER MARK got ill, we lived on the Government benefits — Sickness and later Invalid's Benefits — supplemented by some part time work and help from friends, family and church members. Although we were thoroughly grateful for the extra help we received, the sum total often didn't stretch far enough to pay all the bills as well as buy food and petrol.

One day there'd been some reduction in the government payment we were receiving, and I was furious. I ranted and whined about it all day to anyone who had the misfortune to cross my path. I moaned at pre-school, I whined at the store . . . I rang so many people about it. . . And then I gave my brother Adam, a non-believer, an earful. Without missing a beat he fired back; 'Well you'd better hope your God looks after you then.'

In a 'change my attitude' moment all I could do was look at him and say weakly, 'Yeah, I'd better... okay.' I'd spent the whole day on a rampage of whining and my non-Christian brother bailed me up with one sentence. Our constant goal was to model

New Testament living to others, and encourage them to rely on Jesus, too. But it was certainly easier said than done.

When Mark's diagnosis changed from 'terminal illness' to 'permanent disability,' I became even more fearful and frustrated about our finances. I had no job qualifications outside of being a missionary and mother. I was sitting at home — looking after a sick husband yes — but I worried people would think we weren't doing enough to help ourselves. And I reasoned if I was going to have to be the family's main income provider in the future, I needed to get started on doing something now, before I got more bad news.

I wanted to benefit not just myself but the girls, so began my career as a swim coach. I worked at a local pool teaching swimming for a few hours a week. I saw it as a triple blessing; it gave us a little extra money, I could take the girls to the pools, where they received free swimming lessons while I taught, and I also received free training to be an instructor.

What I hadn't counted on was how an apparently simple little step like that could get me in a tangle with social welfare authorities. I'd understood WINZ – Work & Income New Zealand, the government office which administered social benefit payments — would need to know about the job, and so I'd tried for months to arrange an appointment with them.

Every time I was paid I had contacted WINZ and attached my pay slip to a letter asking for someone to get in touch with me to explain how the payment affected my benefit. I was relieved when after three canceled appointments, I finally met with our new case manager. Because it was such a small amount of money, she advised it would not affect our benefits, but it did make a difference to the $149.50 a week Family Assistance package we received, an adjustable extra payment given to all parents supporting children.

Our case manager informed me they would need to assess how my pay would affect this payment, and that would require the payment being stopped for four weeks while they processed a new application making allowance for the money I received from my swimming job. That was all very well for the bureaucracy, but how on earth were we going to survive without the $600 we'd been relying on for the next month?

The manager suggested I start studying, but then advised that WINZ would only pay for Mark to retrain because he was the principal person on the Invalid's Benefit. Normally after a good sleep things looked better to me, but not this time. I was on the verge of 'losing it' after the WINZ meeting. I kept trying to reassure myself that everything would be alright, but I failed. The yoke on my shoulders had just got a ton heavier.

I agonized over whether I should continue working for a small amount each week and deal with the loss of money from Family Assistance for a month, or quit and just carry on as we were. This wouldn't have seemed like such a big decision if life was normal, but life wasn't normal. My plate was already overloaded, and I was feeling so weary.

I was struggling to see God's hand in all this and yet I knew He had been so faithful in the past. I didn't want to grumble, but it felt like a very lonely battle. I had also noticed I felt jealous of people who were happily married and who had a husband who looked after them. The situation was decided for me by my swimming employer, who summarily changed my terms of employment, and announced the girls were no longer allowed their free lessons.

That would mean I would have to pay someone to look after them while I taught swimming. That just didn't make financial sense. I was also sick of being cold and tired, so I quit. I had a short break and then moved on to work as a part time church receptionist during the day while the girls were at school. After around five years living on a benefit, I was driven by the idea that people would think I was not pulling my financial weight, but I was a mess.

I only managed to keep going with the receptionist job for six months, but it was a critical six months, because it meant I was earning a reasonable wage when I applied for a small mortgage to buy our third home. The loan was approved, but I was worn out. Not long afterward, I finally gave myself permission to be a full-time Mum looking after a sick husband and four daughters. It finally dawned on me that Mark was much sicker than I'd wanted to acknowledge to myself or others, and once I'd looked after his needs there was nothing left over for an outside job.

House No 2

Bible commentators say the seventh of the Ten Commandments — 'Honor your father and your mother, so that you may live long in the land the Lord your God is giving you.' (Exodus 20:12) is the 'first commandment with a promise' attached to it. You do this and you will enjoy certain benefits.

When we moved out of the 'cutest railway cottage in the whole world' in May 2001, it was into a beautiful brand new, three bedroom home with internal access to the garage and no stairs. These were all features we needed to accommodate Mark's wheelchair, which the railway cottage lacked. And we knew from the start God was all over it. First, we were only able to finance it because we'd been obedient to our parent's wishes and taken out life insurance and income protection insurance when we'd purchased the cottage.

This gave us a foundation to keep paying for the cottage and building some equity in the property even after Mark had been forced to stop work. In one of those strange twists life throws at you, we'd gotten a second boost which allowed us to move to the next level in real estate: we received an early payout on Mark's $200,000 life insurance. Once again, the weirdest good things were coming out of a horrible situation.

On the advice of our good friend Matt who was a mortgage broker, we'd become aware this was a possibility. We'd put in a claim with supporting medical documentation which was sent to overseas specialists for consent. It came back approved within a week. Yet again we'd had it confirmed, Mark was going to die. He had to sign a form saying he wasn't going to apply for life insurance again, and the money was ours.

Our shopping list for the next house required it to be closer to the girls' school so they could walk there; have three bedrooms; be on one level and wheelchair friendly; and have a bathroom suitable for modification for a disabled person.

There were two houses that fitted this prescription, and the first we saw was nice enough. But when we walked into the second, we were stunned. In addition to our 'must list' it had a beautiful kitchen, an en suite off the main bedroom, a double garage and security alarms. And it was sparkling, brand spanking new. Our first thought was 'Can we afford this?'

The real estate agent explained the house had been built 'on spec' and had been on the market for nearly six months without selling. 'The owner has dropped the price on it today,' he told us, and we chose to believe him. We thought, 'How *God is that*?

This house was built for Suzanne and Mark' and we lived there for the next four years.

CHAPTER EIGHTEEN
MOUTHS OF BABES

'To be a Christian without prayer is no more possible than
to be alive without breathing.' - Martin Luther.

OUR FOUR GIRLS could hardly be unaware of Mark's illness,
with his very obvious presence in the house and his capacity as a
fully contributing member of the family dwindling as they grew.
And because Mark and I had resolved right from the outset to
include them in everything that was happening, they knew their
Dad was terminally ill.

They'd just learned to accept and cope with all that happened
around them, including his frequent seizures. Our black humor
helped us handle some of the more bizarre incidents.

The girls developed a little game when Mark had his 'pause
seizures.' They would say they were 'leaving a message' and when
he regained consciousness, they would ask if he remembered
what they'd said. Sometimes he could, and so the girls had this
little private joke, a family 'code' of 'I'm leaving a message' for
him like he was an answering machine.

Emerald had only been seventeen months old when Mark
was diagnosed with his illness, and hadn't really known her Dad
as a completely well man, but they enjoyed a natural, innocent

relationship where she would corner him and browbeat him into playing Barbie dolls with her. He had nowhere to run or hide, and he usually graciously obliged.

For Misha and Bonnie, older and more aware of their Dad's decline, it was harder to observe and accept what was happening, but most of the time, real life swept them along. Their daily preoccupations and little rivalries were often the thing that took precedence in their days, more than the long-term question of what was happening with their Dad.

They shared a bedroom in the 'new' house, and as they grew older it became a battle ground. They bickered and argued over who had messed up the room, who was wearing what item of clothing, who was going to the other's side of the room and anything and everything two pre-teen sisters could argue about.

I noted in my journal at the time: 'This home is still a very normal home with children who need to learn to live together. Misha and Bonnie have been fighting so much about their room. They share quite a small room; it fits two beds, one set of drawers and two tiny desks and that's it. But this is only a three bedroom home so there is no choice unless one of them wants to move outside to the playhouse.

'I have told them they can pray about this as God does care for all of our needs, but I have reminded them that I absolutely love living down this driveway, and I love the neighbours. Plus we have the special disabled bathroom for Daddy in this house, so the likelihood of us moving is incredibly slim. But at least if they pray, it becomes God's problem not mine.'

The issue of the bathroom was a major one. We'd had a Government-funded modification done to the bathroom in the new house to accommodate Mark's wheelchair and install handrails by the bath and toilet. The rules stated — quite reasonably — that the government would only pay for a bathroom modification like this in one home, so the idea we could just keep moving houses and have the bathroom remodeled at government expense was a 'no go.'

Between The Cracks

Once Mark's health status changed from 'terminal' to 'permanently disabled,' we moved into a whole new zone. As word spread that Mark wasn't going to die anytime soon, another blow fell. Our lovely South Auckland Hospice nurse came to tell us we were being taken off the Hospice's books. They no longer considered Mark as 'terminal' or as a cancer patient, so we were no longer entitled to their services.

I had not called on them very often, but their emergency support had been so fantastic when I needed it. I could call them 'after hours' — at the weekend or late at night — when Mark was having seizures or severe pain and get free doctor's advice on the best action to take. Once when I completely ran out of morphine, my brother Adam drove to the Hospice Clinic to pick some up for us.

Being 'dropped' by the Hospice felt like yet another blow to someone who was already severely wounded. For me, just the fact that they were no longer there as a backup at night and weekends was huge. Also our neurologist and oncologist had both maintained Mark's condition as terminal, and they considered he still had cancer. I asked myself if this was some warped version of being healed.

With the stress I began to experience recurring chest pains, but I told myself I just had to accept my lot in life. I said to myself: 'SUZ – this is it! Get over the fact you want other things and want life another way! I said to the Lord, 'I need light in this darkness.' For some reason all I got was thicker darkness. As Job 30:26 says, 'I looked for light but darkness fell.'

But I should have been reminding myself that God knows the end from the beginning (Isaiah 46:10) because the most amazing blessing came to us from the change of health status to permanently disabled. Lawyers had advised us that ACC (Accident Compensation Corporation, the government body that administers accident compensation) might accept Mark's illness as a medical mishap.

If it did, we might be able to receive a little more assistance with equipment to cope. We had no idea if ACC would accept the claim. We were stepping onto an invisible path that only Jesus saw. I did however have the weirdest peace about it all.

We went for medical assessments and the months rolled on. We'd all but forgotten about it when we got the most stunning news: we were going to get a substantial financial payout because it had been accepted that Mark's brain damage was the result of a medical mishap from radiation therapy. The money was enough to pay off our mortgage, pay all our outstanding bills and order a decent family computer, as well as put some money aside for the constant unexpected needs every family experiences.

What truly blew me away was about three years before, when we were staying in Rotorua with Neil and Rachel, I felt really strongly that God was asking me to start praying for my mortgage to be paid off. I even came out of my room and told Mark, Neil and Rachel about this prompting from the Holy Spirit. It seemed like an impossible thing to pray, but as we know 'all things are possible with God.'

Every now and then I would even go to the mailbox and look to see if there was a big cheque waiting for me. Three years later, God answered this prayer through this very unexpected payout. Thank you, Jesus!

Pleasant Land

The amazing provision did not stop there! Not long afterward, I was chatting to one of our lovely neighbors on the Right of Way. Shane told me he was moving with his disabled wife Lorraine to Dargaville, a town north of Auckland because they wanted to escape 'the rat race' that was city life. They would be looking to sell their home, which had been built for Lorraine (who was wheelchair-bound with multiple sclerosis), sometime next year.

That morning in my prayer time with the Lord I had read Psalm 16:6, 'The land you have given me is a pleasant land. What a wonderful inheritance!' I had noted in my journal: 'I don't see that pleasant land yet Lord, I still feel very much in the desert. But I have faith and hope that it will come.' Now Shane was telling me his house had three bedrooms, but there could be five, because there was also an office and a second lounge upstairs. By this time I was kind of thinking, 'Wow! This could be the answer to the girls praying about not having to share a room.'

I went home saying to myself; 'God this is amazing; it's practically next door, it has better accessibility for a wheelchair than our present home, and it could be our answer to the need for a bigger home, but there are a few things I want, too. I'd like a kitchen that is double the size of my present one, plus a wood burning fireplace. Lord if you could please provide those extra things as well, I will know this is your provision for us.'

The next day I went to have a look. I walked into the kitchen/dining room area and the kitchen alone was three times bigger than mine and it was beautiful, with a massive wooden bench with tongue and groove cupboards and drawers. I walked around the corner and there was a wood burner. How amazing is our God! Their study could easily be a fourth bedroom and upstairs, a second lounge would be ideal for a playroom and the girls' sleepovers.

The disabled access bathroom was better than the house we were in and was beautifully fitted with tiles and a wooden vanity. To add to the incredible blessing of this house, there were other things there that only God knew I had always wanted. One was a gas cook top and the other a fully covered deck area. I loved everything about it and right then and there asked Shane and Lorraine if I could buy it. We settled on a great price and because of the ACC payout we could afford to buy it. It meant I would have to get another mortgage, but it would only be a small one.

Over the next few months I addressed the challenge of getting our house ready to sell and putting it on the market. There was not much to do, just some painting around the doors and replacing flooring in the bathroom and the toilet areas. Shane offered to help with putting a concrete path around the house, because the shell path was hard to walk on, and difficult to maintain. I was really excited about this new home, although it seemed overwhelming doing it on my own with a sick husband and four little girls.

However, within a few months, with help from friends like David and Lisa Walker, we had painted and repaired the house and sold it. We set up the new home in our Thousand Hills Trust because Mark and I were so overwhelmingly aware it had been given to us by our God who 'owns the cattle on a thousand hills' (Psalm 50: 10). We felt we could take no credit at all for owning this house. It was all God's doing.

CHAPTER NINETEEN
PUSHED TO MY LIMITS

'Hope itself is like a star - not to be seen in the sunshine of prosperity, and only to be discovered in the night of adversity.' - Charles H. Spurgeon.

EVEN BEFORE we moved house, I was feeling overwhelmed and trapped. I had rung WINZ to ask what I was entitled to if I stopped working and went back on the Invalid's Benefit so I could stay home and look after Mark again. But they told me we would effectively lose $70 a week from our budget, which was a huge drop for us, so I decided I should look for a job with fewer hours. I knew I was going to have to start paying a small mortgage on our new home, so I gave myself a good talking to and tried to convince myself I just needed to adjust my attitude.

There was so much to be thankful for in regards to my job, I told myself: The hours were 9:00 a.m. to 3:00 p.m. — perfectly fitting the girls' school day. I didn't have to work school holidays. I had free afterschool care available for the girls if I needed, and my boss was really flexible with my comings and goings. He was understanding on the rare occasions when all the girls were sick at the same time and I had to take time off. I was actually earning enough to meet our needs. While there may have been nothing left over for extras, our basics were being met.

Then in my quiet time I felt I'd received a bit of a 'wake up' call: Matthew 5:48 says, 'In a word, what I'm saying is grow-up. You're kingdom subjects, now live like it. Live out your God created identity. Live generously and graciously toward others, the way God lives towards you' (MSG).

I noted in my journal: 'Well I've just been told, haven't I? God is calling me to grow up this year and my times of visiting my 'self-pity tent' are definitely shorter. Thank you, Lord, for this verse and for giving me a kick in the butt!' But a month after we moved into our new house, I could feel myself crashing both physically or mentally.

Human Strength Ends

The extra stress of selling the house and getting the trust and wills and mortgage organized for the new property had worn me out, and I just could not continue to work at the level I was working. I felt so ridiculously tired I could barely think straight. The adrenaline that had carried me through the last six months of buying and selling houses came to a screeching halt and my brain seemed to have shutdown. And Mark was on his own planet, one where selfishness reigned supreme. He seemed unable to think of anyone else.

I was yelling at Mark and the girls all the time, and wherever I turned I felt there were a million jobs to do. I felt weighed down with physical weights, my body felt so heavy. And sometimes my brain was so foggy that I felt as if it stopped functioning, even in the middle of a conversation. I would be chatting on the phone and my mind would just stop; I couldn't focus or even recall what I intended to say next and I'd be forced to hang up. I began pleading with God to sort the situation out; I didn't know how we would cope financially if I left work.

Then it seemed as if my stressed state might also be affecting the girls. Just as they were leaving for school one morning, Bonnie burst into tears. She had no idea what was wrong, so all I could do was walk her to school holding her hand. That seemed to be all she needed. I walked back home in a daze and before I left for my receptionist job — late again — I rang Belinda and said, 'I don't think I can do this. I'm not doing anything well.'

After our staff meeting the boss asked to talk to me. I walked into his office and sat down. He looked at me across his desk and very compassionately asked how was I doing. I decided honesty was my best option and said, 'I can't work anymore, I am so tired, I can't think, and everything at home still needs my attention as I am the only functioning adult.

'Mark is still very sick and this has been hard on him and his mother Val, too, as each day he has to get ready and leave the house after his shower lady (the paid staff to assist Mark) comes. I pick him up from his parents after work, but the moving between both houses is exhausting him. Then I said words that required so much faith; 'I'm sorry but I think I am going to have to resign.' It felt so good to have made the decision. I realized as I sat in my boss's office that I needed to make my girls, Mark and my home a priority.

I did feel nervous, and asked myself: 'Am I making the right decision? Lord, please confirm it to me.' A famous evangelist George Mueller once said, 'Faith begins where man's power ends.' I'd resigned because I felt I had come to the end of my own ability to carry on, but I had no idea how we were going to meet the shortfall in the family budget that would result. There was no doubt we needed some power beyond us to carry us through. I was going to have to trust God for the shortfall. If I imagined I would at least regain my serenity by reducing my workload, I was in for another shock.

Panic Attack

Stopping work turned out nothing like I expected. As soon as I relinquished the reins of control, I fell apart. I went down straight away with the flu, and then I started having panic attacks. I was only able to do the bare necessities around the house. If I managed to get the washing out and back in, folded and put away I thought myself the biggest hero.

Home was my refuge. The panic attacks occurred when I left my safe little house, to go to the pharmacy, the supermarket or the bank. Typical of my upset state was the day I went to the bank to withdraw money for bills. As soon as I walked in I started shaking. When I tried to fill in the withdrawal form, I couldn't remember the date. I started frantically looking for the date to put on the slip . . . but I couldn't find it. I had a chorus going in my head 'where's the date? It has to be somewhere in this stupid bank. . . goodness, why is the bank hiding the date from me? Oh there it is, why is it so bloody small, I can hardly see it, do they think we are all Superman with super eyesight? Stupid bloody bank'

I managed to make it to the teller and then as fast as I could, I got out of there and quickly drove home. I couldn't breathe. I have never had an attack like it before and I felt totally freaked out. So I just hid away in my nice safe house as much as I could.

CHAPTER TWENTY
THE GAME OF THE ROYAL WAY

'I had discovered that when God supplied money He did it in a kingly manner, not in some groveling way.' - *God's Smuggler*, Brother Andrew.

TOO MANY days over the coming months I wished I had never got out of bed. For the first time in my life, I had stress-related chest pains. Every breath hurt and the longer I didn't breathe properly the more it hurt. I felt beyond desperate. Sometimes we saw miracles. Many times I had to hold onto faith when little seemed to change. But over the long haul, we were amazingly blessed. It was just very hard getting through the 'long haul.'

Occasionally I had a strangely disassociated sense of looking at my own life from outside. While we'd been busy selling one house and buying another, Rob Harley had interviewed us again, for *Life Stories,* a DVD series aimed at people who have 'hard' questions about how God works in tough real-life situations.

Our story was included in a series titled *Where Is God When It Hurts?* and Rob asked me to come and speak at its launch screening. The first thing that came to me as I was watching this re-telling of our lives through someone else's eyes was what a sad story it was — and then it dawned on me, it was our story. It was mine.

Brother Andrew, the missionary evangelist who became famous for smuggling Bibles into Communist countries during the height of the Cold War recounts many 'miracle episodes' of God's provision to him when he was in training in Glasgow. He considered God had a sense of humor over money and came to regard the way his divine King took care of his material needs as 'The Game of the Royal Way.'

After reading his book I made a conscious decision to have more faith for the little things. Brother Andrew was convinced, 'God as King' will provide in a royal way for all our needs, not just the huge ones. And Isaiah 41:10 says, 'I've picked you. I haven't dropped you. Don't panic. I'm with you. There's no need to fear for I'm your God. I'll give you strength. I'll help you. I'll hold steady, keep a firm grip on you' (MSG).

As I noted in my journal at the time: 'Dear Jesus, my God, my husband – thank you for all my many blessings – my girls, my family, my home and my friends. Thank you, Lord, that I am learning to trust you in a real personal way every day for the little things. Please provide. I pray that as your bride I start living in a royal way in my mind and in my actions. I pray my words and actions will be seasoned with grace.'

Then 'real-life' would intrude. My journal from October 18, 2005 shows a journey I went on that included finances, faith and strangely enough, hope: 'We have quite a list of physical needs that I am looking to God to provide for us. They include a $180 credit card bill, and new summer school shoes for all four girls. We have been invited to a birthday party and I need to buy a present and the cats need flea powder. Please heavenly husband, provide for these needs.

'I was talking to Mark about how everything is scary – the future, finances, everything. I went on to list some of the scary things I have been thinking about. Is Mark going to be like this for twenty years? Is he going to get worse and be harder to care for? Is he going to have a long yukky death?

'It's all scary. It's scary if he does die and it's scary if he doesn't.

'The sun was streaming into my bedroom early this evening and I lay on the bed to enjoy it. The Bible was beside me and I closed it and randomly opened it. It opened on Matthew 6. I was disappointed because I know that chapter quite well and yet I felt compelled to read it.'

Matthew 6:32–34 says, 'People who don't know God and the way he works, fuss over these things, but you both know God and how he works. Steep your life in God-reality, God-initiative, God-provisions. Don't worry about missing out. You'll find your everyday concerns will be met. Give your entire attention to what God is doing right now, and don't get worked up about what may or may not happen tomorrow. God will help you deal with whatever hard things come up when the time comes' (MSG).

'Thank you Jesus for your clear word. You are not saying it isn't scary, but you are reminding me that I know you, and I know how you work. My role is to keep my focus on you.'

Intensive Training

A few days later, I looked at our finances and we had enough to buy groceries, but nothing else. So God hadn't yet provided for the additional needs. The Lord led me to a verse in Matthew 15:28, 'Jesus gave in. "Oh woman, your faith is something else. What you want is what you get!"' (MSG).

The rest of Matthew 15 was about Jesus healing the lame, the maimed, the blind and dumb and then feeding four thousand people. I prayed: 'You are the God of many miracles. May you say to me, "Suz, your faith is something else – what you want is what you get." And so my father, my king, my husband, I believe for your provision for my daily needs today.'

While I was living through the tough stuff, I was also invited to speak at different meetings. I had an engagement at a North Shore church, and I was hoping for some recent miracle I could share with them. I didn't want to be 'just another guest speaker.'

I wanted to share what God was teaching me. I wanted God to use Mark and me to help people change their lives. I prayed, 'If I am just going to be another nice speaker then I would rather not do this. Father, I feel like my insides are going to burst from not being able to express what I want. Use me, flow through me, speak through me.'

By 22 October there was still no material change in our circumstances. God had not provided for those needs. But I had also been led to yet another verse on people of faith found in Acts 6, 'Stephen, a man full of faith and the Holy Spirit brimming with God's grace and energy, wisdom and spirit. When he spoke his face was like the face of an angel!' I was inspired all over again that God was calling me to be a woman of faith.

In Brother Andrew's book he observed, 'I could believe God for toothpaste and shaving cream but not for $15,000'. I thought that was interesting since I could believe for thousands of dollars, but not for the little every day needs. I prayed God would help me to stretch my faith so I would know that He provided for the daily needs, not just extravagant items. With the birthday party imminent, I needed something nice to wear.

October 23: So yesterday did God provide the money? No! Belinda and her Mum lent me some nice clothes to wear and I made a voucher on the computer to take my friend out for lunch for her birthday present. So I guess He provided in a way.

I know God can and will provide but I am sick and tired of living by juggling every cent and praying for everything, and then God doesn't really provide – He makes do. As far as I am concerned, He did not provide in the royal way that I believed He would yesterday. I do feel let down and I feel exhausted. What's worse is how do I find the money for Bonnie and Emerald's birthdays and Christmas?

Another two days went by, and I had to put the girls' summer school shoes on our credit card because I did not have the cash to pay for them. I hated going into debt. In an act of defiance I bought myself two pairs of shoes as well.

I felt like I was saying to God; 'Well now, not only do you have to pay the credit card for the girls' school shoes but also for my shoes, too.'

October 25: I was praying this morning during my quiet time and looked at the scripture God gave me. Isaiah 7:11, 'Ask for a sign from your God. Ask anything. Be extravagant. Ask for the moon!' (MSG). Lord, the sign I ask for is that you do provide our daily needs. I would like to be given $500. A sign that my future is going to be good – that you come miraculously and help me get ready for my speech on Sunday, that I will be a vessel of the Holy Spirit speaking the very words of God. And please show me that my future is going to be amazing.'

October 26: This morning, when I was preparing for what I was going to say on Sunday, God totally blew me away by showing me what He had been trying to teach me over the last few weeks about being a woman of great faith. The great faith that He was encouraging me with in those two scriptures (Matthew 15 and Acts 6) was not for the finances, but to be a woman of great faith and to have hope. To have hope, I have to have faith. Faith to believe my hope for the future is going to be good. I am beginning to understand that to hope is to be obedient to God.

Here I was focusing on being a woman of great faith by believing for money to buy shoes and a birthday present, and the whole time God was trying to get across to me that I needed to have faith my future was going to be good – to hope for that future. I have forced myself to not think about the future and not believe that it will be good because of the stupid illness, but God is saying loud and clear, 'You are a woman of great faith, now use that same faith to hope!' WOW! So the Lord taught me a lesson and I am going to share this when I speak on Sunday.

Bathed In Blessing

October 31: My Sunday speaking engagement has just blown me away. The congregation was so encouraging and after I spoke I got to talk to lots of people. But the most surprising thing was what God did through the church. We were given an overwhelming amount of groceries; boxes and boxes of food. We could barely fit it into our car and our friends' cars.

But the blessing didn't end there. When we were unpacking the food at home we found envelopes taped to boxes. At the end of it all, including the money the church had given me for speaking, there was the grand total of $500 cash – the exact amount I had prayed for as a sign the other day. Isn't God truly amazing?!

And to top off the day, Jasmine had gone to the Sunday school class and they were encouraged to write a prayer for what they needed. Jasmine showed me later she had written a prayer for God to provide groceries for us. So as you can imagine, she has been buzzing ever since God answered her prayer straight away and so abundantly.

'Jesus you have gone over the top (OTT) on the blessing thing, WOW, thank you so much. I am going to be able to get everything I prayed for and pay the credit card off. You have provided for every need and then some. THANK YOU!'

CHAPTER TWENTY-ONE
THE GOD OF THE SMALL THINGS

'In the same way, wisdom is sweet to your soul. If you find it, you will have a bright future, and your hopes will not be cut short.' - Proverbs 24:14.

THE GIRLS' needs were always at the top of my priorities list. As with Jasmine praying for food for the table, they all, at various times, directly experienced God's provision in remarkable ways. We saw all sorts of daily miracles for small things. One was simply from anonymous giving. Different people at different times would commit to giving us a regular financial gift ranging from $20 to $100 per week. The amazing thing about these gifts was they never overlapped. When one person or couple ceased giving, soon after someone else would come to us and say God had asked them to give to us for a time. God's economy and God's timing were impeccable. These gifts were always requested to be undisclosed, so it was not generally known who was giving what and when. We just shared with people that God was providing continuously – because He was!

Miraculous Provision

Misha needed new shoes and I told her 'you need to pray honey, I have no money.' She prayed and the next morning we went out the front door and just inside the porch there was a shoebox with $100 in it.

Misha and Bonnie both needed braces because their teeth were very noticeably out of alignment, at a cost of $5,000 each. I knew this was an expense we couldn't afford but I really felt to not limit God in what He can do. He was and is a God who cares for all things and longs to bless us. So with that in mind I decided to make the necessary appointment. On the ride home from the orthodontist, I was very quiet as I contemplated how I was going to find $10,000 for teeth. But I reminded myself God is amazing and He cares for my girls more than I ever could and so I was not going to doubt that He would provide for this. I thanked Him in advance for his provision.

Within a few weeks we saw the most amazing miracle for these braces. I had managed to pay an initial deposit of $400, leaving a monthly payment of $266. I worked out from my savings from Mark's life insurance I could spare $3000 to pay straight away and then the monthly payments would be $180.

So I prayed, 'Okay God all you have to come up with is $180 more a month.' Soon after I got a letter from the Government Department of Family Assistance, advising that our payments were increasing by $90 a fortnight — $180 a month. The exact amount for the orthodontist's bill. How amazing is our God!

Over the next couple of months we diligently paid but even with the extra aid from Family Assistance our finances were tight. So I continued to pray for God to cover this need. After our documentary aired on the national channel TV3, Rob Harley the director had a phone call from a person who wished to remain anonymous enquiring if we had any outstanding bills. Rob called us and I mentioned the orthodontist's bill. Rob asked for the exact amount owing and within a week we were sent a cheque covering the whole bill. I stood there in shock at the generosity of strangers and the goodness of our God to provide for <u>all</u> things, not just our daily needs.

Credit Card Settled

Occasionally, over the years when we had no income at all, we used the credit card and then paid it off diligently with any spare cash we had. We'd used it for a deposit on a dining table and chairs before Mark got sick, and then just kept chipping away paying it off. At one stage we owed approximately $1100 on it. For no particular reason I rang the bank to check on the balance, and the bank officer said it was '$1900' — I naturally presumed in debt.

I went into shock. I had no idea how this had happened. Perhaps someone had illegally used our card? Practically hyperventilating I asked the bank staffer to start reading through the withdrawals and deposits. (We didn't do online banking in those days.)

And then she said, '$3000 deposit.' I said, 'What . . ? No, there hasn't been any $3000 deposit.'

'Yes' she said. 'A $3000 deposit on such and such a date.' And then I realized we had $1900 in credit. And I remembered that sometime previously I'd had a call from the church office and they'd said, 'someone has asked for your credit card number' and I just had not given it another thought.

I was breathless during the whole conversation, first because I thought we'd somehow gotten hugely more in debt than

I'd planned, but then discovered someone had given us this wonderful anonymous gift. It was another huge miracle.

Tale Of A Sofa

To backtrack a little: When Mark started radiation therapy he was sleeping a lot, and I didn't want him isolated in our bedroom. I wanted a nice big sofa for him so he could still be in the midst of family life with the girls even if he did nod off. I started praying for a couch which would be big enough to accommodate him comfortably and allow him to sleep in the living room. We had $300 in our budget, and it was before the days of on-line trading, so I was looking through lots of second hand stores, but I just couldn't find anything that seemed right.

Then one Tuesday it was my turn to take Mark to his radiation therapy and on the way home I decided to browse the Freedom Furniture store (it's my favorite!). Mark slept in the car after his treatment while I found just what we needed — a nice sofa module and chaise combination. I sat on that couch and I talked to God. I said, 'God this couch is $2400 and I have $300. I want this couch and I want it in green. I'm going to get this couch in green.' Forty-five minutes later I was still sitting on the couch talking to God. The sales assistant had approached and asked if I needed any help and I'd just said, 'No thanks, I'm considering buying this couch.'

Mark woke up from his nap, came looking and found me sitting on the couch. I told him; 'I am getting this couch.' He asked; 'How much is it?'

'$2400.'

He gave me with one of those 'you're dreaming!' looks and reminded me; 'Honey we have $300.'

I replied, 'Dear Jesus I want this couch.' I went home and I just prayed. I said, 'I am being a bit of a spoiled brat. I don't need this couch, but I want this couch.'

Six weeks later we got a cheque from friends in the US which turned out to be exactly the right amount for the couch minus our $300 when it was exchanged into NZ dollars. Mark slept through many a day on that couch with his kids playing around him, and I thought often 'How cool is our God?'

All the way through He wasn't just limited to our needs, He gave us our wants, like a nice new Freedom Furniture couch. I learned God supersedes us. When He is first in our finances He supersedes our needs.

Amazing Wheels

Mark and I had been out enjoying a lovely lunch with one of our close friends, Holly, when Mark began to suffer one of his 'long slow' seizures. We headed back to the car to get him home, and as I was slowly and painfully trying to get him settled into the front seat, I noticed the most amazing disability vehicle was parked beside us. The woman owner and I got chatting, and she showed me how the whole back of the van raised and lowered and a press-button automatic ramp lifted the wheelchair into a safe position.

This little incident got me thinking. ACC had offered us a disability vehicle in the past, but we had thought it unnecessary. But now that Mark was so much sicker I was wondering if I should request one to make things a whole lot easier for both of us.

After taking about twenty minutes to get Mark into the car and load his wheelchair into the trunk and even longer to get him unloaded when we got home because his body was now shattered from the seizure, I was convinced it was time to inquire about a disability vehicle for Mark. My thinking was something like: Mark is supposed to be like this for years to come so I might as well start the process.

Within a week of my initial inquiry, our amazing case manager rang to say an occupational therapist would be coming to assess our needs so we could start the process for applying for the vehicle. Mark's illness had progressed to the point where a normal week was what we used to call a bad week. He now had frequent seizures; he needed the fast acting morphine more often and he often felt nauseous. Within a few weeks of the occupational therapist's visit, we went to a car yard to try out different vehicles. I never knew there was such variety.

Poor Mark was pushed and pulled in and out of about six vehicles, and I was the one who had to push and pull him in and out of those vehicles. We had to practice seeing which van he would fit in height-wise. We had to practice which ramp was wide enough for his wheelchair. We had to practice if I was strong enough to push him up this slant of a ramp or a lesser slope. We had to practice trying to put him into a side door wheelchair access or a back door access. We had to practice whether he would be more comfortable in the back of a van or in the middle of a van closer to the front.

We had to see if we could fit the six of us in the van with Mark in his wheelchair. Oh my goodness – I had no idea. But our occupational therapist and the car dealer together pretty much worked out what would be perfect for Mark and the family. The request went in to the Accident Compensation Corporation.

One Year Later

November 6, 2008: Today we went and picked up Mark's new vehicle, an amazing Toyota Alphard. The whole back of the van lowered and a ramp came down automatically for us to push Mark up and down. There were doors on both sides and you could just flick the handles and the doors opened automatically. It was a dream to drive even though it was big, but it didn't feel big. Mark's wheelchair sat behind the front passenger seat so he was near me if he needed me, not like some disabled vans that have the person sitting in the very back. What he liked most was the air-conditioning vent was right at his face level.

The vehicle included six seats, so if Mark ever wanted to sit in a seat and not in his chair the whole family could still fit in. God you are so incredibly good to us, thank you and thank you for an amazing country that looks after its own.

CHAPTER
TWENTY-TWO
SILVER LININGS

'You never really know a man until you understand things from his point of view, until you climb into his skin and walk around in it.' - *To Kill A Mockingbird,* Harper Lee, 1960 - taken from a saying of the Cherokee tribes.

JOE SOUTH and Elvis Presley both had popular hit records with the country song *Walk A Mile in My Shoes.* Its plea for racial tolerance and compassion — derived from the famous Harper Lee novel — has been covered by many other artists since, from Bryan Ferry to Lena Horne and Coldcut. We often gave thanks for the relatively generous New Zealand social welfare system, but we certainly came to understand better than most what it meant to rely on a Government Benefit for our very existence.

In our eight years of desperate illness we gained an intimate view of how the less fortunate lived. I found it constantly depressing and I had to fight not getting wound up and anxious by the lack. I questioned how those in government could think that the assistance they gave out was anywhere near enough, and I understood it wasn't surprising many beneficiaries felt desperate about their lives. I had to fight feelings of envy, watching those who were physically able to get ahead without a weekly struggle.

There were some weeks we had $20 left over for food after the other bills were paid.

When we began living on welfare at the start of Mark's illness, it was very tight and required careful budgeting, but with some windfall gifts from family and friends it was possible. Nearly eight years later when we moved off a benefit, it was nowhere near enough to support a family of two adults and four growing teenagers.

The only way we came through it well and living in a beautiful home was because we trusted God with our finances and were obedient to His word. And the hard reality was, we managed to get off the benefit because things just kept getting worse for Mark. We were still singing the same song — *Every cloud has a silver lining. Or it's an ill wind that blows nobody any good.*

Ironically we got off a benefit because Mark got so ill that a new case manager, who specialized in serious injury cases, assessed I could be paid as a full-time caregiver under Accident Compensation provisions.

The basis for that was that Mark required twenty-four hour care, and if I wasn't doing it, he would have to be cared for in a full-time residential facility. After our case manager spent two and a half hours with us, seeing how our home worked, she said she didn't think there would be a problem with the application as Mark definitely needed full-time care and that was what I had been doing anyway.

It would mean quite a bit more money, which would be a great blessing. When they finally came back to us and said the change of status had been approved, it felt like the 'miracle of miracles.' I was to be paid for eighty-five hours a week and Val, his Mum would be paid for twenty hours weekly relief care.

The hours were worked out on the basis that I cared for Mark twenty-four hours a day, seven days a week. Although it was paid at a minimum hourly rate, because so many hours were involved, it resulted in a big improvement in our situation. Because it was set up so I was employed by a home help agency, they dealt with all my tax payments. God is so good. He said to believe for His financial provision, and I am amazed at what He has done in a way I never imagined.

Always There

There is not one person on this planet who is not affected by money. For some it is their security, their warm blanket – their god. Others require simply enough to live life comfortably and they are generous with their excess. But for far too many people, money is their constant stress; and they are always facing the questions: 'How will I feed my children today?' 'How will I buy my child a warm sweater?' 'How can I afford school books?'

It is an age old problem and one that unfortunately will not go away, but I have learned our God is a God who provides! Our God is a God who is generous! Our God is a God who blesses us beyond anything we can ever imagine! All we have to do is surrender our all to Him.

For some this is too big a price to pay. But it is the price Mark and I had willingly paid before we were even married. It is a price I still pay. I have tried my best to be wise with the money that the Lord has provided for us either from wages, benefits or other sources. And God has never failed to provide where there has been lack. Sometimes the blessings and answers have not come how I wanted or the way I thought would have been best. But God has never let us down.

Hebrews 3:5-6 says, 'Don't love money; be satisfied with what you have. For God has said, "I will never fail you. I will never abandon you." So we can say with confidence, "The LORD is my helper, so I will have no fear. What can mere people do to me?"'

So although I don't have many answers, I do have the authority to say God is there, God is good, God will not fail and God is God because that is what I have learned and that is what I have undoubtedly experienced.

PART IV-
GOD'S WAYS ARE PERFECT*

Despite Appearances, Cancer Does Not Have The Last Word
(2 Samuel 22:31)*
(2008 – 2009)

CHAPTER TWENTY-THREE
A NEW WAITING GAME

*"'Welcome, Prince,' said Aslan. "Do you feel yourself
sufficient to take up the Kingship of Narnia?"
"I - I don't think I do, Sir," said Caspian. "I am only a kid."
"Good," said Aslan. "If you had felt yourself sufficient, it
would have been proof that you were not.'"*
C.S. Lewis - *Prince Caspian.*

IF THERE was one thing I learned from my years of journeying
with Mark's illness it was that I was definitely 'not sufficient'
without God's strength to get through even a single day. I had
battled with God for seven years wanting – indeed demanding -
that He change things to my liking. I had finally come to a place
of accepting He was in control and His ways were perfect. I was
even finding peace and comfort in that surrender. I'd undergone
some sort of 'Divine Extreme Makeover.'

I was like Humpty Dumpty in the children's Nursery
Rhyme. I'd 'sat on a wall and had a great fall,' but unlike 'all the
King's horses and all the King's men' God in his graciousness
was willing to put me back together again. The old 'wants' still
occasionally tugged and I still thought of our lives as our 'stupid
situation.' But I'd found some joy in giving up and taking the

attitude of 'Whatever God, you are God so I guess you have it figured out and it will be great.' I may not have liked it, but Mark's illness and my caregiver role had become 'the new normal.' Then our world was rocked to its foundations by another unwelcome change.

A month after the eighth anniversary of Marks' original diagnosis of brain cancer, we were again awaiting results from an Auckland Neurology Clinic MRI scan. Mark had been having a series of really bad days, even for him, so his doctors decided an MRI might be in order to see what was going on in his brain.

I had already phoned the clinic to ask if his results were in and had been told rather rudely that 'if anything had changed you would have been contacted.' So it came as a shock when I opened an Auckland Hospital letter expecting to find confirmation of the nurse's verbal advice and instead found this from Dr Anderson:

'Dear Mark and Suzanne,

Re: MRI Results

I tried to call you both today but unfortunately you weren't home.

Unfortunately, Mark's scan shows a new abnormality which looks like a recurrent tumor, but at a different site from previously.

It is difficult to be certain given that he has such widespread radiation-induced damage. Nevertheless, there is a clear change compared with the previous scan. . .'

What? How? Where? We were both in shock. A new tumor, in a different area of the brain? This was totally not what either of us expected. The letter went on to say Mark had another appointment in three weeks to go over the scan. We drew our own conclusions: Three weeks is quite a while so it's obviously not very invasive. . . Three weeks to wait to see, to find out where the different site is, and how big it is . . . It is going to be a long three weeks.

I suggested to Mark that we keep the latest development quiet, except for close friends and family, until we had seen Dr Anderson. He agreed. He cried as he put into words what we were all thinking; 'Does this mean I'm going to die soon?' I replied, 'Honey at this point we know so little, let's not worry about what we don't know yet. God says He will take care of our tomorrow so let's put it in His hands for now.' Mark nodded his head. For a married couple that were so close before this illness, we were so far apart in this journey.

I couldn't imagine what he was processing, or how he was dealing with the fact that regardless of size or place, he had another tumor growing in his brain. Once again something was invading him and he had no control over it. And a new tumor most likely meant death was closer. I could not walk this very lonely road with him and he could not walk this very lonely road with me because they led to two completely different places.

End in Sight?

The next day I woke up and for the first time in years, I considered there could be an end to this illness, an end to looking after an invalid husband. The mix of emotions running through my heart and mind drove me crazy. Half of me was going 'NO! Mark needs to be here to watch his girls grow up, he needs to be here for me to talk to because he is still my best friend, he can't go.'

The other half was going – 'Yes, no more watching Mark get sicker and sicker; no more having to see him in pain; no more running to get morphine; no more running to get a bucket because he is about to throw up; no more wheelchair;

no more pee on the floor; no more endless waiting because he is the slowest person on the planet.' And then I thought – 'oh my goodness it is so terrible you are thinking like that, Suzanne.'

But the truth was I was thinking like that. I was so tired of what the illness brought – the endless caregiving that I was expected to do twenty-four hours a day, seven days a week. Both options were equally horrific – death or life like this. Except for Mark, death would mean going home to be with Jesus in heaven. Death would mean complete healing and wholeness on the other side of eternity. So the death part was only horrific for us, left here with the empty hole he would leave.

All the girls were matter of fact about the news, and I guess in a way that was our reality. There might have been a new tumor, but it didn't change anything about how we lived. That grinds on. Once again I turned to the 'Good Book' for comfort: Psalm 49:5, 15, 'There is no need to fear when times of trouble come…But as for me, God will redeem my life. He will snatch me from the power of death.' Despite this news, our family did not need to fear and ultimately God had the authority even over death – how cool!

No Need To Fear

Mark had been in quite a bit of pain and he was not sleeping much, which was actually a real nuisance. When he was awake and up I couldn't leave the house because he was unsafe. And when he was up, he constantly wanted me to do things for him like get him the TV remote, get him another drink, help him up, get him pain killers, charge his iPod – can you tell I might have had enough of this? One week till the neurology appointment.

June 1: As I was praying this morning, God told me to read Jeremiah 9:20-21, 'Listen, you women to the words of the Lord, open your ears to what he has to say. Teach your daughters to wail; teach one another to lament. For death has crept in through our windows and has entered our mansions. It has killed off the flower of our youth: Children no longer play in the streets and young men no longer gather in the square.' I think the Lord might be preparing us that this tumor is going to mean death. What an incredible prophetic word to be given by the Lord.

June 4: Mark is starting to freak out about the appointment and the confirmation of the tumor and so now I am starting to freak out, too. Belinda told us a calming technique where you breathe in saying, 'Jesus' and breathe out saying 'is Lord.' So both Mark and I are doing that.

I said to Mark, 'You cannot freak out, imagine how the girls will cope if they see you freaking out. You need to spend time with Jesus and He needs to be your strength, I can't be your strength because I need Jesus to be my strength too.'

Eight years of appointments, and every one of them delivering seriously bad news. I think both of us are over them. The whole experience of coming out of the appointment devastated, and then starting the long journey back to learning to cope with each day in the light of more bad news. And here we go again.

7 June: We have asked Mark's Dad, David, if he would like to come with us to see the doctor. We are so anxious about it, we arrive early. When we are called in, Dr. Anderson gets straight to the point. The scan comes up on the computer screen and the new growth is clearly visible. It is on the right hand side pushing into the middle of his brain at the back. It is not huge like the first tumor, but it is not small either. Dr. Anderson explains that it is very unusual for a completely new tumor to grow on the

other hemisphere of the brain and in another area. Mark's first tumor was on the left hand side of the brain at the front.

Mark asks, 'Do you think it's malignant?' Dr. Anderson answers, 'Without a biopsy it is truly hard to say and the fact that it is nowhere near the original site of the first tumor increases the uncertainty, but it is definitely a lesion of some kind that wasn't there before. The options are surgery to get a sample to biopsy or we wait and do another MRI scan in about six weeks and see if it has changed or grown. What would you both like to do?'

I look at Mark's face and without even having to ask him I know what he prefers: 'Surgery is not an option; Mark would not cope with that. We would like to wait and see what a second scan shows in a couple of months.' Mark is nodding furiously. We leave knowing little more than we arrived. What we do know is the growth is not huge and not going to cause his death any time soon. We do know it hasn't been growing for a long time because Mark has had semi-regular brain MRIs. Most importantly, we know God is in control of this family and our lives.

God knew that new lesion was growing and He knows what is ahead. I have such a sense of peace about it all. As to our daily life – what we saw changes nothing. Mark is still very sick because of the radiation necrosis, and I still have to look after him.

Jeremiah 10:6–7 says, 'Lord, there is no one like you! For you are great and your name is full of power. Who would not fear you, O King of Nations? The title belongs to you alone! Among all the wise people of the earth and in all the kingdoms of the world, there is no one like you.'

That is the God who is control of my life. I have no need to fear what this life holds. I only need to have an awesome and holy fear of Him.

CHAPTER TWENTY-FOUR
HEARING FROM GOD

'If you don't like something, change it. If you can't change it, change your attitude.' - Maya Angelou.

JUNE 9, 2008: Talk about a delayed reaction to the news. Today I was so grumpy and had no patience with anyone, especially the girls. I yelled at them constantly and the language that was coming out of my mouth was most unattractive. God, please help me live this out walking in the fruit of the Spirit, which is 'love, joy, peace, patience, kindness, goodness, faithfulness, gentleness and self-control' (Galatians 5: 22). Please help me not to get angry over dumb things and to get my priorities straight.

God showed me that part of my anger is because I am scared to watch the girls grieve. When they start to get upset I say to them; 'Well it's not happening today.' But the Lord has said to me that I have to allow them to grieve because they have to process that their Daddy has another lump growing in his head. Lord, help me to do that and give me the wisdom I need to parent them through this new situation.

Physically, Mark is not good. He had such severe pains last night that they turned into seizures. It was horrible to witness, let alone for Mark who had to endure them. I ask: Lord, lead me to a scripture that I can pray over Mark and myself during this very uncertain time: 'You will keep in perfect peace all who trust in you, whose thoughts are fixed on you!' *(Isaiah 26: 3)*. Thank you Lord!

My Favourite Thing

Sometimes when I speak publicly I preface what I am going to say with an amusing item that makes all dog lovers chuckle and is so true of dogs — if our dog Charlie is anything to judge by. It goes like this:

The Dog's Diary

8:00 a.m. - Dog food! My favorite thing!

9:30 a.m. - A car ride! My favorite thing!

9:40 a.m. - A walk in the park! My favorite thing!

10:30 a.m. - Got rubbed and petted! My favorite thing!

12:00 p.m. - Milk bones! My favorite thing!

1:00 p.m. - Played in the yard! My favorite thing!

3:00 p.m. - Wagged my tail! My favorite thing!

5:00 p.m. - Dinner! My favorite thing!

7:00 p.m. - Got to play ball! My favorite thing!

8:00 p.m. - Wow! Watched TV with the people! My favorite thing!

11:00 p.m. - Sleeping on the bed! My favorite thing!

Dogs, some animal psychologists suggest, are 'stuck in time' and mainly live in the present — hence their rolling feast of 'favorite things.' I, on the other hand, have found it very hard to live in the present, and I have only ever had one favorite thing, and that is Jesus. My life has been devoted in one way or another to developing and maintaining a relationship with Jesus and the

Holy Spirit, the comforter He sent to earth to be with us after His crucifixion.

But all these years of being a caregiver had left me battling over my purpose on this planet. Just what was the point of Suzanne Pamela Holmes nee Wotherspoon being on this planet? Aside from giving birth to four beautiful girls – I could really see little point. Was it really to just look after Mark all these years? If so, what was the purpose of Mark's life? It was especially hard because after years of illness Mark was content to sit or sleep and that drove me crazy, and so I yelled at him— a lot. I could not understand why he didn't try to still make something of his life. Since a very young girl my heart had been set on fire by the instruction every believer is given in Matthew 28:18 to 'go and make disciples of all the nations.'

It's like it is the energy to my day, my mind and my purpose. For me nothing has ever been of more importance than telling everyone that Jesus is the way in this life and to our eternal life in heaven. Since Mark's illness has consumed our days, I have seemingly lost the ability and time to do this very thing that gives me purpose to each day.

Thankfully though, God still talks to me in a variety of ways – though dreams, through prophetic words from other close Christian friends, through faith challenging books, and most especially from studying the word of God for so many years. As I have time to reflect on the hard years of Mark's illness, I am amazed to recall just how many different ways God makes Himself known to us if we invite Him to speak to us and want to hear from Him.

Prophetic Words

It was the middle of February and the weather was perfect. I had shared a beautiful lunch with friends and after we'd eaten we prayed for each other. I received a couple of very encouraging prophetic words as others prayed for me. The first was that as a teenager I had prayed, 'God my life is completely and utterly yours, use me in any way you want,' and God was keeping me to that prayer.

The second was God saying to me, 'Do not despise what I am doing in your life.' One of the women had a vision of me walking on a path littered with sharp stones, scorpions, snakes and other dangers and impediments. As I moved I was forced to stand on painful things. I was looking up at God, crying and protesting 'this hurts so much.' In my friend's vision, God was crying, too, at what I was going through. But He was encouraging me that I needed to walk this painful path to be able to have His glory shine through me and able to be used by Him to tell others about Him. My friend could sense God's overwhelming and incredible love for me. He was holding me and was completely in empathy with my pain. He was hurting too at what I was going through.

I was completely captivated by these insights, and I had walked with a new, slightly unfamiliar appreciation of God's love for me. What a restful place that is. I know things aren't going to get any better, but I knew Jesus was walking this path with me and loving me through it. I had a lovely peace in that.

Wheelchair Dreams

Not long after the lunch, I had a strange dream. I was pulling Mark along by the handle on one side of his wheelchair in a dense fog, so thick I could not see ahead, beside or behind us. It made no sense to be pulling him from the side of his wheelchair, but that was what I was doing and obviously we weren't getting anywhere. Then out of nowhere, without warning, a big rig smashed into us. Mark died instantly, and I was tossed in the air like a rag doll, right through the rig's front windscreen, where I landed, totally unharmed, in the passenger's seat, continuing my journey as if this collision had never occurred.

The significance of the crash with the truck escaped me, but I did feel I was groping towards understanding the first part of the dream where I was trying to, ineffectually, pull Mark along in his wheelchair. It seemed to me that increasingly I was trying to encourage and even push Mark to engage more: in his spiritual life with God, in his relationship with his girls and in his general involvement with life — and it's about as effective as pulling a wheelchair by the side arm.

I knew he was always tired and he was on so much medication that it made him sleepy, so it was hard, but I still tried to push him to live. What's interesting was since those words were spoken over me at that prayer lunch, I was no longer in a rush for this time together to end. I realized each part of the journey was training and molding me and replacing some of my selfishness with a sense of God. I felt more at peace than ever, even if it was a slow, painful and seemingly futile process. In I Corinthians 13 God says to trust steadily, hope unswervingly and love extravagantly. Could I do that? Please, Lord, help me to trust you, hope in you and love you, Mark, my girls and others extravagantly.

The Living Word

One of the most consistent and effective ways God speaks to me is through His word. Hebrews 4:12 says, the word of God is 'living and active. Sharper than any double-edged sword, it penetrates even to dividing soul and spirit, joints and marrow; it judges the thoughts and attitudes of the heart' (NIV). That is my experience of the word too, almost on a daily basis. Psalm 1:2 calls us to 'delight in the law of the LORD, meditating on it day and night.'

I have done that for many years, and now the word comes to my mind whenever I feel a need for guidance. This is how it works:

It is September 2008, and I took the family to the movies. Mark is so very slow and not seeming to think things through. I was trying to get him in the car, and I had to keep telling him what steps to take. 'Get into the car Mark and sit down.' He would just stop as if he couldn't think of what the next step was. It is agonizing to watch, and it is agonizing to care for because I just get frustrated so quickly.

When I finally fell into bed at the end of the day, I turned to my reflective time. I said; 'Lord, it is bedtime and I would love a scripture from you.' Solomon prays when dedicating the new temple — quoted in 2 Chronicles 6:14, 'O Lord, God of Israel, there is no God like you in all heaven and earth. You keep your promises and show unfailing love to all who obey you and are eager to do your will.'

I too, am so eager to do your will, Lord and obey you. What are the promises you have given me? And the promises of God just flowed from me, the promises I have prayed and meditated over all these years:

You will be my husband.

Hosea 2:16, '"When that day comes," says the Lord, "you will call me 'my husband' instead of 'my master.'"'

You provide for me and my family.

Matthew 6:31–33, 'So don't worry about these things, saying, "What will we eat? What will we drink? What will we wear?"' These things dominate the thoughts of unbelievers, but your heavenly Father already knows all your needs. Seek the Kingdom of God above all else, and live righteously, and he will give you everything you need.'

You protect me.

Psalm 91:1–4, 'Those who live in the shelter of the Most High will find rest in the shadow of the Almighty. This I declare about the Lord: He alone is my refuge, my place of safety; he is my God, and I trust him. For he will rescue you from every trap and protect you from deadly disease. He will cover you with his feathers. He will shelter you with his wings. His faithful promises are your armor and protection.'

You bless me.

Haggai 2:19, 'I am giving you a promise now while the seed is still in the barn. You have not yet harvested your grain, and your grapevines, fig trees, pomegranates, and olive trees have not yet produced their crops. But from this day onward I will bless you.'

You anoint me to tell people the good news about you Jesus, to comfort the broken hearted and to set the captives free.

Isaiah 61:1, 'The Spirit of the Sovereign Lord is upon me, for the Lord has anointed me, to bring good news to the poor. He has sent me to comfort the broken hearted and to proclaim that captives will be released and prisoners will be freed.'

You publish your glorious deeds, which I believe is the writing of my journal.

Psalm 96:3, 'Publish his glorious deeds among the nations. Tell everyone about the amazing things he does.'

You give us a good future filled with hope.

Jeremiah 29:11, '"For I know the plans I have for you," says the Lord. "They are plans for good and not for disaster, to give you a future and a hope."'

You enable me to accomplish infinitely more than I could ever ask or hope.

Ephesians 3:20, 'Now all glory to God, who is able, through his mighty power at work within us, to accomplish infinitely more than we might ask or think.'

You show me your great love.

Ephesians 3:18–19, 'And may you have the power to understand, as all God's people should, how wide, how long, how high, and how deep his love is. May you experience the love of Christ, though it is too great to understand fully.'

You forgive my sins and make me new.

Psalm 51:10, 'Create in me a clean heart, O God. Renew a loyal spirit within me.'

And you will blow my mind with what you have in store for us here on this earth and in heaven.

1 Corinthians 2:9–10, 'No eye has seen, no ear has heard, and no mind has imagined what God has prepared for those who love him. But it was to us that God revealed these things by his Spirit. For his Spirit searches out everything and shows us God's deep secrets.'

Through Friends' Books

My dear friend Holly Robertson came and spent the day with us. She shared from Tricia McCary Rhodes' book *At The Name Of Jesus*, (Bethany House) on how Jesus can become an obstacle to our faith when he does things that we consider out of character to our expectations. The section on 'Jesus The Stumbling Block' cried out to me.

Jesus is likened to being a 'stumbling block' in Romans 9:33, 'Behold I lay in Zion a stone of stumbling and a rock of offense, and he who believes in Him will not be disappointed' — and I could relate to it because that's what caused me to fall a few years back, after Mark's radiation necrosis diagnosis. At that time I was thinking Jesus – where was He? He was challenging all my thoughts about Him.

Tricia McCary Rhodes writes that every serious believer has to come to terms with the truth that being a follower of Jesus 'means to grapple with the offensive, illogical ways of a God who won't be hijacked by human reasoning no matter how religious its overtones . . . To follow Jesus is to walk a path that will often not make sense to the natural mind.'

It's taken me so long to realize that God is not like Santa Claus and He is not some 'sugar-daddy' Father in heaven. He is the Almighty and very mysterious God of the Universe. He is an unboxable God who will never fit into any preconceived ideas we have of Him. He is God!

I was reading Exodus 26 on the exact measurement, the materials and instructions God gave the Israelites for building the temple. Which made me think – if God did that for a material dwelling place, is He that particular when making us into 'his dwelling place' according to the exact design that He has planned? And then God led me to the passage in Job 23:13, 'But he is singular and sovereign, who can argue with him? He does what he wants, when he wants to. He'll complete in detail what he's decided about me and whatever else he determines to do' (MSG). I guess that answers that question.

Prisoner In The Third Cell

I was chatting on the phone to my long-time friend Sheila Mark in Christchurch, and she recommended a book to me that she had just read, a book called *Prisoner in the Third Cell* by Gene Edwards (Tyndale House Publishers Inc.) It is based on the verses found in Luke 7:18–23 which tells the story of John the Baptist in prison sending his disciples to Jesus and asking, 'Are you the Messiah or shall we expect someone else?'

Jesus had just done an amazing miracle. He encountered a big funeral procession coming out of the village of Nain, where a widow's only son was being borne on an open bier, and Jesus stepped forward and stunned everyone there by raising him to back to life. In New Testament terms it was 'instant fame'; everyone was talking about the 'great prophet' while His cousin John the Baptist languished in prison, missing all the action. Maybe John felt left out, and momentarily needed encouragement or reassurance that Jesus was worth dying for.

Jesus gave a surprising response. I would expect him to say something along the lines of 'of course John, I can't believe you have to ask that question.' Instead what he says in Luke 7:22–23 is, '"Go and tell John the things you have seen and heard: that the blind see, the lame walk, the lepers are cleansed, the deaf hear, the dead are raised, the poor have the gospel preached to them. And blessed is he who is not offended because of Me"' (NKJ).

What does that really mean? Look at what I've done John and you are blessed if you aren't offended by me, even though you are in prison? How does that make sense? The Amplified Bible puts it like this: 'And blessed (happy, fortunate, and to be envied) is he who takes no offense at Me and finds no cause for stumbling in or through Me and is not hindered from seeing the Truth.'

Gene Edwards explains we are blessed if we are not offended or upset or questioning of how God does things and what He allows in our lives. So I am blessed despite complaining about Mark's illness, I accept that God has allowed it (not that God has done it to us – big difference) and I am not offended or upset, annoyed, repelled or even made to question or stumble in my faith. That really got me thinking.

God Speaks Through Movies

On my thirty-eighth birthday, I took the whole family to see *Prince Caspian*, the second movie in the Narnia series. For some unconscionable reason, I got really upset at the end, where the two oldest children, Peter and Susan, are told they will never return to Narnia, where they had lived for many happy years as Kings and Queens. I was perplexed as to why it had affected me so greatly.

And then the parallels with my own life hit me. I had been forced to relinquish a dream. I had been in a very happy place I loved and had wanted to stay there. And I, too, had it taken away from me and told I could never go back. Our happy marriage, our ministry, our traveling, my children's father, my dream of my comfortable future with Mark – this was my happy time, and it had all been taken away and would never return. I realized I needed to replace the old dreams with new ones.

Birthdays have always been important to me, so the wound smarts even more the next day when no-one remembered it was my birthday. The girls were all little horrors getting ready for school. In protest, I opened a tin of tomato soup for dinner, because I refused point blank to cook my own birthday tea. I recalled the birthday not too many years ago when Mark made a twelve-hour train journey from Dresden to Warsaw where I was staying with Misha and Bonnie — both under three at the time — just to be sure he was home to surprise me on my birthday. And once again I took up my daily conversation with the Lord. I talked (and continue to talk) to Him as an intimate friend.

'Jesus,' I said, 'I give you full permission to heal this very raw wound. Please replace the old dreams that I hang onto, which can never be reality and replace them with new dreams that come from you and will one day be reality. I ask this in your mighty name Jesus.' As if to answer that plea, I sensed the Lord leading me to Isaiah 41:13-16, 'I am holding you by the right hand – I, the Lord your God and I say to you, "Do not be afraid, I am here to help you. Despised though you are, O Israel, don't be afraid, I am here to help you. I am the Lord your redeemer. I am the Holy One of Israel.

'"You will be a new threshing instrument with many sharp teeth. You will tear all your enemies apart, making chaff of mountains. You will toss them in the air; and the wind will blow them all away. A whirlwind will scatter them. And the joy of the Lord will fill you to overflowing. You will glory in the Holy One of Israel."'

And I replied, 'Thank you Lord, you are holding me, you are helping me, I am not to be afraid of the future, and you have promised that the joy of the Lord will fill me to overflowing. That joy will replace this hurt. Thank you, Jesus.'

CHAPTER
TWENTY-FIVE
WE HAVE BEEN IN A VALLEY

'Pray as if everything depends on God, work as if
everything depends on you.' - attributed to Ignatius Loyola.

AS 2008 drew to a close, I had to be more vigilant than usual
with Mark's care. He was very tired, he fell more often, and he
had also been doing this weird thing, of choking on nothing.
He would gag trying to take his pills and his water. For people
watching from the outside Mark did not seem much different.
But to me, the one who watched him for all these years, he was
slower in all ways.

After years of warring with God about not wanting to be a
caregiver, I was now almost okay with it. You are God! You are
Almighty! You are 'I AM'. And I accept. No further explanation
is needed.

I heard a quote from the Vineyard Movement pastor John
Wimber (who also battled cancer). 'I have been in the valley
and the view isn't so bad.' Although it took a while (a very long
while) my vision had adjusted and the view wasn't as bad.

Look at what the word of God says in Job 12:10, 'In his hand
is the life of every living thing and the breath of all mankind'
(NIV). What a great place for us all to be – in the hand of the

Almighty. Maybe His hand is the view I see from now, which is why it isn't quite so bad. Or look at Acts 3:19, 'So repent, change your mind and purpose, turn around and return to God, that your sins may be erased, blotted out, wiped clean, that times of refreshing , of recovering from the effects of heat, of reviving with fresh air may come from the presence of the Lord' (AB).

I guess in a lot of ways this is what I have done. I have repented of my terrible temper tantrum at the Lord. I have chosen to read the Bible and through that change my mind and purpose. With that, God has cleansed me and times of refreshing have come.

Wow, it's not till I have taken a step back and looked back at myself that I have been able to notice how I have changed. I am not this warring crazy person – I admit I still have my days, absolutely, but there is a definite change.

However, there are still days that I am mad, still days that I cry in sheer frustration and still days I swear and yell. And there are days of worry. Mark is definitely slower, and I don't know what that means. Is the necrosis still spreading? Is the tumor growing? Or is this just a bad few weeks and he will pick up again soon?

I turned to John 16:33, 'I have told you these things so that in me you may have perfect peace and confidence. In the world you have tribulation and trial and distress and frustration, but be of good cheer (Take courage, be confident, certain undaunted) for I have overcome the world. I have deprived it of power to harm you and have conquered it for you!' (AB).

In November, when Bonnie turned fourteen and Emerald turned ten we felt blessed Mark was there for yet another birthday, despite the fact that he was extremely hard work. I was very happy he was there for his gorgeous daughters.

Cancer Denied Last Word

I guess from the outside looking in people see us as a defeated family, and Mark as a defeated man, but they are only seeing the physical aspect. Cancer has not had the last word in this family.

Mark has accepted Jesus as his Lord and Saviour and although the body he is in now fails him, he is headed for an eternal home with God. God has overcome any power this illness had over us, particularly me. The power that sought to rob me of a relationship with the Creator, and the power that sought to make me a bitter, angry and resentful person, has not won.

Amazingly with all my frustrations, I can still walk in peace and contentment, knowing that whatever this life brings, He is God and He is in control and has it all sorted. Yes, from the outside looking in we are in a sad situation.

But from the inside that is my daily experience, we are closer to God than we ever would have been. I will take courage, I will be confident and I will be undaunted by all this because Satan has been deprived of the power to conquer us. When Christmas comes I go all out to celebrate with the family — Mark's Mum and Dad and mine too — at our house.

We have the house and table covered with Christmas decorations including festive serviettes and Santa hats that at my insistence everyone except Val dutifully wears. There is lots of chatter and laughter. I love having everyone together. I wish my brothers and their families could be here. Mark is in his wheelchair at the table, with his Santa hat on (he has no choice but to wear it.)

We have already opened our gifts, which was a crazy mess but loads of fun. I want to make sure we get a family photo of the six of us with our Santa hats on, that will be cool to have as a memory of this lovely day.

On New Year's Eve I reflect that another whole year has passed. There are moments I have wanted Mark dead and all this finished and over. There are moments I have wanted desperately for him to be healed and restored, but mostly I see I have learned more and more contentment and with that there has come peace.

In Philippians 4:6–7 it says, 'Don't worry about anything; instead, pray about everything. Tell God what you need, and thank him for all he has done. Then you will experience God's peace, which exceeds anything we can understand. His peace will guard your hearts and minds as you live in Christ Jesus.'

I am starting to understand what that peace feels and looks like in my life. It brings with it a comfort that I had previously lacked and it also opens the way for more of God's love to shower upon me. I can do this life; with Jesus I can actually do it better than I have done. But only through Jesus because I have fully seen the mess I make when left to my own emotions and devices. Eight years, nine months – I am a very slow learner!

Odd Acceptance

I entered 2009 feeling more relaxed about the coming year than I had for eight years. Life had settled into a rhythm of normality, although it may not have been everyone's normal.

Misha was fifteen and about to start the first of the important last three years of high school. In New Zealand these years build on each other. To progress and eventually gain university entrance, each student must pass the previous year's exams and study requirements. Bonnie was fourteen and entering her second year of high school. Jasmine was twelve and in her last year of intermediate (middle) school. Emerald was ten and a year away from entering middle school.

I have been Mark's caregiver for so long that the days when we were very much in love and extremely happy are a distant memory. I often wonder if my grieving over the loss of my husband had already happened through the years of his illness.

But I have real moments of terror at the thought of Mark dying and gone for good. On one of these occasions I had such a strong physical reaction through my whole body I keeled over in intense pain.

I had to quickly thrust the panic aside and remind myself that God says we only need to worry about today, and that Mark is a long way from dying. I told myself it will not be something I will have to experience any time soon.

It was a revelation I was not in any way prepared for his death. And then God reminded me not to be afraid. No matter what I face, He is with me. Jeremiah 30:10 says, 'So do not be afraid, Jacob, my servant; do not be dismayed, Israel, says the Lord.' And Isaiah 43:1–2 reinforces, 'But now, O Jacob, listen to the Lord who created you. O Israel, the one who formed you says, "Do not be afraid, for I have ransomed you. I have called you by name; you are mine. When you go through deep waters, I will be with you. When you go through rivers of difficulty, you will not drown. When you walk through the fire of oppression, you will not be burned up; the flames will not consume you."'

CHAPTER
TWENTY-SIX
A STRANGE CLOUD DESCENDS

'You used to be much more..."muchier." You've lost your
muchness.' - Lewis Carroll, *Alice in Wonderland.*

FEBRUARY 25, 2009: Belinda reminded me of something very
interesting today. 'You were the one who always said, "It'll be
great" and now instead, you're the one often stressing out. You
never say that anymore.' That is totally true. I always used to say
about everything; 'It'll be great!' We often used to laugh and say
I should have 'It'll be great!' as a personalized number plate, but
I never say it now.

I realized I don't think like that anymore, and I feel saddened.
A lot of my optimism and joy at life has gone. It has slipped away
so slowly I didn't notice, but regardless, it has gone. I guess living
with the consequences of long-term illness dampens the human
spirit.

March 6, 2009: We have had another bad day with Mark.
He was so unsteady on his feet that he fell down hard, but
thankfully I was in the way, so he fell on me and not the coffee
table.

The girls and I picked him up and got him into bed. I
turned around to see Misha helping her sisters and making sure

everyone was okay. She was trying so hard to be strong for her sisters and me, and I am trying so hard to be strong for everyone.

I think I need to have a chat with them all and say we need to cry when we need to cry and be sad when we are sad. There is no escaping this sadness, but I think I need to give everyone permission to show their feelings instead of putting this brave face on for everyone else in the family, which is what we are all doing. As Job 36:15 tells us, 'But by the means of their suffering, he rescues those who suffer. For he gets their attention through adversity.' That is the truth, God truly does get our attention in the midst of our suffering.

Heavy Waiting Game

April 28, 2009: A strange atmosphere has come over our home. I haven't been able to put my finger on it. It is unwelcome but it has descended and it seems set to stay. Without prompting, each of us starts to wonder; what is the point of life, when all it does is end? The conversation in my home takes on an interesting but depressing turn. The girls start to want fewer people around them. Misha is finding everyone annoying. I am about to turn thirty-nine and wonder 'Is this it?'

The first part of my life was exciting; growing up, falling in love, planning a future, having children, and then, all of a sudden, the thought lands on you with a bang; 'is this truly it?' Was I meant for more? I wonder am I having some early midlife crisis, but then I realize my teenagers are saying the same things. It's quite startling coming from a fifteen-year-old.

Then this morning the Lord let me in on what was taking place. We are hanging around waiting for death. The new tumor was found nearly a year ago. We have tried to play the waiting game, and we were successful when we were diverted by other family events like my brother Adam and Raelene's recent wedding. Now all the entertainment of the wedding and family visits is over. Without realizing it, we have started on a downward spiral.

And the stress of it all is having negative repercussions on my daughters. How could it not? When I attend Misha and Bonnie's mid-year parent teacher interviews I am shocked to get a bad report from their teachers the majority of whom say my girls are naughty and disruptive in class and never do their homework. They apparently interrupt the class and divert attention from the teacher's set tasks. At which I thought to myself, 'Well I am not sure why they aren't harnessing their obvious leadership abilities.'

I have come away quite dumbfounded. Am I so entrenched in looking after Mark that I am not noticing what is going on with my girls or that they are not doing their homework? Is the stress at home with Mark's illness and new tumor causing my girls to be disobedient at school? I don't know, and I really don't know what to do.

This family is barely coping with what we have to deal with. I wonder how many other fifteen and fourteen-year-olds have to run to get a bucket for their Dad when he yells, 'I'm going to throw up.' Or have to give their Dad morphine when his pain is bad, or help their Mum clean up their Dad's pee when he has had an accident, or stroke their Dad's back when he is having a bad seizure, or cut up his food for his meals, or plan for his death and funeral? I'm guessing not that many, and with all that in mind, I actually don't give a toss what those teachers think!

Six Will Be Five

The girls and I have almost come to a mutual though unspoken agreement that we need to start facing up to the reality that Mark is most likely going to die; we still have no idea when, but a tumor is growing.

Mark's eyesight is deteriorating and his childish behavior is escalating. Sometimes it is very hard to ignore. It is obvious that subtle changes are occurring in his brain though we don't know exactly what they are.

We are in waiting for another MRI and that is the big problem. We are waiting. Waiting for an MRI, waiting for the news of what is going on in his brain, waiting for his illness to take more control and for Mark to get worse and ultimately the six of us are hanging around waiting for death.

It is little wonder that I am starting to hate waiting. I even think I hate the word. Why do we say waiting? It gives the impression of sitting and being inactive while something inevitable happens. Why not say we are 'journeying towards death?'

At least that makes it feel like we are doing something, like we are going somewhere with purpose. It might not be the destination we picked, but regardless, it is where we are headed and so we will journey together to it. How much more positive and uplifting does that sound? Even I feel encouraged.

The next question arises: what exactly do you do when you are on a journey with someone toward death? It's not like swords and fighting are involved, but it is a sort of battle, a battle of the mind to stay positive, alert and strong. So, do we carry on life as normal or do we make extra effort no matter how tired we feel to make the time we have special? Something to remember with a smile? We should try to laugh more – but how, I wonder?

I need to make an effort to plan things to look forward to and positive events to focus on. And not only that; the Bible says in Psalm 118:24, 'This is the day the Lord has made. We will rejoice and be glad in it.' So I figure God has made every day and there must be reasons we can rejoice in it. I will attempt to make an effort to look for them and be thankful for our whole family's sake.

Let This Cup Pass

May 29, 2009: Mark and I have received the results of the MRI he had eight days ago. The tumor has grown significantly since the last MRI just over a year ago; 10mm or more in all. It is also showing up much more clearly in the scan. Dr. Anderson said both of these things are indicative of a malignant brain tumor. So aside from doing brain surgery to get a biopsy and finding out for certain, it looks like cancer.

I am not entirely sure how I feel. Of course this is not a complete surprise, but it is still confirmation of something terrible. For over nine years Mark has been sick and now we are definitely looking at an end, though nothing seems definite.

Brain tumors are incredibly unpredictable. Part of me wants this illness over, to stop having the stress of looking after someone. Part of me still wants to wake up one morning and Mark be completely healed, but I do not believe this is going to happen anymore.

Part of me completely freaks out at what death will look like and mean to us. It is such an unknown, something I have never walked with someone so close. So how do I feel? Probably the best answer is: I have no idea.

Jesus says in John 18:11, 'Shall I not drink from the cup of suffering the Father has given me?' Actually Lord, if it's all the same to you I would really like this cup of suffering to be over. I would like to have some joy in my life and my family's life.

When Mark turns forty in September I cannot believe he has really made it. Actually I am pretty sure no one believes it. We had a lovely dinner party for him with some of our dear friends, as well as David and Val on the Saturday before his birthday.

As 2009 draws to a close, we valiantly strive to maintain normal lives. Misha begins driving lessons to get her motor vehicle license. We decide to get a Christmas puppy to help bring life and laughter to our sombre household. Sometimes I pause long enough to be grateful that Mark is seeing his eldest daughter as she hovers on the cusp of adulthood.

However, underlying our joy is something that feels very like fear. C. S. Lewis wrote in *A Grief Observed* 'No one ever told me that grief felt so like fear.' And each of us in our own way probably understands what he is talking about.

CHAPTER
TWENTY-SEVEN
BEYOND MY CONTROL

'Death ends a life, not a relationship.' - Mitch Albom,
Tuesdays with Morrie.

DECEMBER 3, 2009: At 5:30 a.m. my alarm sounds. I stagger out of bed to make a coffee and climb back in still trying to wake up. I start to read my Bible. I have been back in bed with my coffee for about two minutes when Mark starts screaming and grabbing at his head.

I look at him wondering 'what on earth is the issue' and then in my completely sympathetic Christ-like way tell him to, 'Shut up, you're going to wake the girls!' Normally Mark would pull himself together and quiet down, at which point I would ask if he wanted some morphine and go and get it for him.

But this morning he doesn't calm. He keeps screaming and writhing around in severe pain. I am tired out; anxiety delays my reaction time, and I find I am momentarily immobilised. I stare at him, not speaking. My mind is whirling with the question 'what is going on here?' I finally managed to ask 'Do you want some morphine?' And then – words I will long regret - 'Can you please shut up?'

I get up to get the drugs and as I look over to Mark's side of the bed, I see it is wet; Mark has lost control of his bladder. There is urine all over the sheets, blankets, and down the side of the mattress and on the floor.

Remembering he wears a bag round the clock I can't quite figure out how this accident has happened. I go into automatic clean up mode and start shouting instructions: 'Mark you need to make your way to the bathroom. I have to change you and get these sheets in the washing machine... will you get a move on ... honestly Mark what a pain, this is a mess... hurry up...' On and on I go.

I pull the sheets and blankets off the bed, while Mark is trying to make his way around the bed to the bathroom so I can change him. He is moving so slowly this morning. . . I give him some morphine. While we wait for it to take effect I continue with the clean up. I am in full speed ahead mode; intent on cleaning the floor, stripping the sheets, cleaning the mattress, getting Mark to the bathroom to clean him. As I rush around I toss him loving comments like, 'Will you hurry up?' 'What a mess!' and the most compassionate of all; 'Honestly, sometimes you are such a pain in the arse!'

With intermittent painful cries, Mark makes his way around the bed very slowly. He has reached the end of the bed and is making tentative moves towards the bathroom as I am heading to the laundry with a load of sheets for the washing machine, when I hear him scream out Bonnie's name. I turn around to see him falling. I drop the sheets and run into Bonnie's room shouting, 'Wake up, your Dad wants you, and I need you to help me get him up, he has fallen over.'

Mark is very limp and very heavy to lift. He seems to have lost all power in his legs. He isn't able to make them obey the slightest instruction. Bonnie runs to get the wheelchair so we can sit him in it and then I can push him into the bathroom to change him. I am focused on his wet boxers; I need to clean him up, but at the same time I am thinking the morphine should have worked by now.

I can't change his boxers while he is sitting, so before I put him in the chair I lean him against the bathroom doorway and get Bonnie to lean against him to hold him up with her back to him looking the other way, so I can pull his underpants off and put some fresh ones on. It's now clear he isn't in any shape to endure a shower right now. Bonnie is holding her Dad up while looking in the other direction, and I am pulling his pants down, but when I ask Mark to lift his leg to remove the pants, he can't do it. It is dawning on me that this is an unusually bad day.

He starts slumping over and we can no longer keep him upright, so I cover Mark up with a towel, get Bonnie to turn around and shift the wheelchair just behind Mark, and then I slowly put him in the chair. I start panicking then; he is sitting in the chair, still moaning and writhing in pain. Half undressed and so limp and heavy, he is unmovable. Then he yells, 'I'm going to be sick!' I jump through the very small gap between the wheelchair and bathroom door and run and get his bucket. I look at the clock and twenty minutes has passed, so I can give him another lot of morphine. I jump through the gap again and race to the kitchen and return with pills.

I lean over Mark and say, 'Honey, here's some more morphine,' sounding a heck of a lot calmer than I feel. Mark yells, 'throw it in my mouth!' My hands are shaking badly as I put the six small tablets in his mouth and then place the bottle of water on his lips so he can swallow them. My heart is pounding so fast I feel like I am running a marathon. I touch

Mark's forehead and it is burning hot. Tears cloud my eyes as I start rubbing his head, saying over and over to him, 'it's alright.'

I yell at Bonnie to get me the phone and I ring Mark's father, David, and ask him to come over as soon as he can. I explain Mark is having a bad morning and I can't redress him; I need some help. As I complete the call to David, Mark's eyes roll back, his head slumps back and his breathing becomes incredibly shallow. I start yelling, 'Mark, you need to breath deeper, like this,' and start mimicking useless big breaths.

Mark is completely unresponsive and now I am in a state of abject panic. What is happening to my husband? This isn't how it goes. Normally the morphine works. I help him get changed and shower him, put him back to bed and our day goes on. The situation is beyond my control. I can handle most things with Mark, but now I am out of my league.

I grab the phone and dial the emergency number. As calmly as I can, I ask for the ambulance. When the operator comes on I start out very calmly saying my husband has a brain tumor and has woken up screaming and now is not responding, but somewhere in the first minute of my explanation I break down. This is not a good day, this is not right, something is very wrong and I need someone to help right now.

As I am talking, I lean over Mark's body which is collapsed in the wheelchair, holding his head up, trying to get him to open his eyes. The operator asks questions about our address, reassuring me help is on the way. She promises to stay on the line until the paramedics arrive.

Mark's parents arrive. I look at them with wide eyes and say, 'Mark is really bad and I don't know what is wrong. I have rung the ambulance so can one of you go outside and make sure they come to the right house?' I stay on the phone with emergency services. My heart is pounding so loudly, my mind is panicking, I have never felt so out of control, or so in the dark. In a short time, in what seems record time really, the St John's ambulance arrives and the paramedics come in. They take over, and I stand back and stare.

I have no idea what is happening, but they are here now and the responsibility isn't mine. Mark is now in good hands and will be fine soon. As much as I have hated this illness Mark has been my best friend for twenty-two years and in six days' time he will have been my husband for twenty years. I can't bear to watch what is happening.

As the paramedics take over, I notice my pyjama top feels wet. It has now been an hour since Mark woke up screaming, and I have been running on adrenaline for that hour. I am drenched in sweat. I need to change before I go anywhere, and I have four daughters standing perplexed and wondering what is happening.

They strap Mark into the gurney and start heading towards the ambulance. I ask David and Val if they will travel with Mark in the ambulance and we will follow behind. My breathing has calmed down to a normal rate and for the first time this morning I don't feel in panic mode.

Mark is now safe and sound with the paramedics in the ambulance headed to the best place for him today; I am convinced he will be fine soon. Emerald comes up to me and asks if she can see Daddy in the ambulance, so we walk together to the back door as they finish securing the bed for the trip.

I put my hands on her shoulders and say, 'see Daddy is all good now.' But as the paramedic closes the door, he looks at me and calmly says, 'I would hurry if I was you.' The ambulance doors lock securely as I stand staring at it in shock: *what does he mean I should hurry? Is Mark really that bad?* I run into the house and start yelling instructions to the girls to hurry up so we can leave as soon as possible.

Then I remember Charlie. We have a tiny puppy that we can't leave all day. Of all things to have to think about right at the moment, it's hilarious really, but I have to work out who is going to look after him. I ring Belinda and Brenton and tell them the situation. They are amazing and tell me to leave Charlie in the garage in his little pen, and they will come and get him as soon as they can.

For the first time in twenty-two years I leave the house without any makeup on and my hair wet from the shower. With beds unmade, drawn curtains, pee-stained blankets and clothes scattered on the floor and buckets of water that I was using to clean up beside my bed, we leave the house in record time not caring at all.

PART V–
TO GOD BE THE GLORY

Unanswerable Questions
In The Light of Eternity
Dec 3 – 2009 – Dec 8 2009

CHAPTER
TWENTY-EIGHT
THE VOICE THAT CALLS

'For I am convinced that neither death nor life, neither angels nor demons, neither the present nor the future, nor any powers, neither height nor depth, nor anything else in all creation, will be able to separate us from the love of God that is in Christ Jesus our Lord.' - Romans 8: 38–39 (NIV).

AS USUAL the freeway is congested with morning commuters and I start praying, 'Lord please give us a clear run to the hospital.' Tossing my cell phone to the girls, I get them to text some friends, asking them to pray for Mark. The CD player is playing worship music and one of the songs declares, 'You are my hiding place, my safe refuge, my treasure Lord you are.' Another prayer, 'Lord be my hiding place and safe refuge today.'

Amazingly the freeway clears and we get to the hospital as the clock strikes 8:30 a.m. As we enter Mark's room, he is lying with a tube down his throat and beeping machines surround him. This is not at all how I imagined finding him. I had presumed he would be given anti-seizure medication and would be waking up soon.

Val tells me that he seems to be asleep and out of pain as they have started a morphine drip. One of the doctors asks to talk to me privately and wants to know if Mark has a 'do not resuscitate' order. I am shocked at the question, but without thinking about the implications of the question answer yes, Mark signed one years ago. I am starting to feel pretty relaxed. Mark is in the best place and he has just pulled at the tube down his throat like he wants it out. I think that is a pretty good sign he is going to wake up soon.

My thoughts flick to Bonnie's surprise birthday party this weekend. It will be such a nuisance if Mark is in hospital. And I recall last time Mark was in hospital — for kidney stones — they did not look after his needs very well. I am going to insist he comes home as quickly as possible because I know I will look after him better. I might be a grumpy old hag sometimes, but I love him, and I try my best to take good care of him.

I remember then that this is the day of Misha's restricted license driving test. I ring John, the driving instructor, fill him in on our day and ask him what he thinks we should do. He is keen for Misha to go ahead, and he arranges to come and pick her up from the hospital and return her after the test. I am a bit apprehensive, but Misha is keen and there really is no point to her hanging around here when she can mark up this milestone. We decide she should go for it. Mark will probably be awake when she gets back and hopefully she will have some exciting news to tell him.

The Funny Side

Our family can never be serious for long. While drinking coffee and eating sandwiches provided by the hospital staff, we joke about the day's events and what Mark will say when we tell him about it all. One funny thing that keeps happening is every time they have to move or lift Mark, they call for reinforcements and say, 'He's a big boy you know.'

When they first did this, Bonnie and I looked at each other and laughed. What were they on about? We had lifted him off the floor by ourselves this very morning. And it hasn't been just once that they have said it. Bonnie and I laugh every time the staff say this about Mark's size.

All of our phones are beeping and ringing with texts and phone calls as word that Mark is in hospital spreads. I keep repeating, 'It's all fine, just pray.' People are also starting to ask if they should come to the hospital, and I keep saying, 'No, don't stress.'

Mark hasn't been in hospital in over six and a half years despite the fact he has been seriously ill. To our friends and family the fact he is now in hospital means something serious has happened, but I am convinced it is all a momentary drama and Mark will regain consciousness any minute.

My Dad seems to have other ideas, and decides to ring my two brothers. He tells Rob, who lives in Te Aroha, about one and a half hour drive south of Auckland, he should come to the hospital if he can. I decide we should let our very good friends Neil and Rachel from Rotorua know of this change as well. They are as close to us as anyone and have been part of this very long journey.

The driving instructor John arrives to pick up Misha; we all give her a big hug and tell her we will be praying for her. She is obviously really nervous about the test and now to add to her anxiety we have this drama.

Unexpected After All

Soon after Misha departs, the doctor informs us the medical team has decided to do a CT scan of Mark's brain to discover what is going on. Mum and Dad take the three other girls to the café to get something to eat and Mark's parents and I follow Mark's bed (as staff wheel it) to the CT scanner. We sit quietly, apprehensive at what it might reveal. We bolster ourselves by agreeing it will be good to find out what is causing the problem.

Once the scan is over, we all trail behind the bed again and head to the ward Mark will be settled in. I notice the ward entry reads 'Palliative Care.' Am I missing something? Isn't this the ward they send people who are going to die?

Time has become a blur and as we settle into the tiniest of rooms, two doctors ask to speak to us. The three girls who are still here, along with David, Val, and I follow the doctors to the family room at the end of the ward and anxiously wait to hear their report.

They tell us Mark has suffered a massive bleed in the area of the second tumor and there is nothing they can do. I ask them to repeat what they have said, to explain it more clearly. Nothing changes the meaning the second time round.

Mark has had a massive brain bleed, his brain is filling up with blood, and there is nothing they can do. I put my head in my hands in unbelief. This can't be happening, this is a bad dream and I am going to wake up any minute.

My eyes start stinging, and my whole body starts shaking – this is really happening! Nine and a half years we had prepared ourselves for dying and death, yet in reality I am no way ready to finally face it. Not only is it here, but for the first time in twenty years of marriage I am facing something massive completely alone. Mark is lying there unconscious, and I am sitting in a room hearing he is dying.

I am not able to talk to Mark about this, hug him through this, pray with him or even yell at him. Mark is on a journey that none of us can walk, and he is leaving me behind, alone. I feel overwhelmed. Mark is dying. I can't believe it. I don't want it. What have I been thinking all these years when I had said I wanted it over? I want to run and hide and not face what is happening.

My whole body is trembling uncontrollably, and I feel like I am having a panic attack. This can't be it. Not now. I had finally given in and relaxed to the notion that this was my life, I didn't love it and it was getting harder, but it was my life. I have actually been excited at our upcoming twentieth wedding anniversary. My brain is screaming, NO!

One of the nurses comes to the family room to tell us Mark is all settled in the ward and we can go and sit with him. We walk in. We all start sobbing. At the age of forty, Mark is dying before our eyes. We all take turns hugging him and kissing him and telling him we love him.

As I look at Mark's peaceful face, I notice a tear slip out of the corner of his eye and slide down his face. I realize he can hear and understand what we are saying, and that breaks my heart even more. Then it hits me with force; those irritated, bossy words I yelled at him this morning were the last words we would ever speak to each other. I am filled with guilt at my impatience and determination to just 'get things done.'

If only I had known that half hour was going to be our last time together, I would have said, 'I love you, and thank you.' Now it is too late.

Triumph In Pain

I receive a text from Misha saying she is back and she has passed her test. She is now a legal driver. I walk to the front of the hospital to meet her, and I can't think how I am going to tell her that her Dad is dying. The doors open and I can see her walking across the car park towards me, smiling broadly, proud of her accomplishment.

I step forward to embrace her to say, 'Well done!' but not a word will come out. Instead I begin to cry. She looks at me and she knows. I hold her and hug her, so proud of my brave girl who has passed her driver's test on the day her Dad is going to die.

Getting back to the room, it is her turn to hug Mark and cry. 'Dad,' she says, 'I passed my driving test; your oldest daughter can now drive.' He is unresponsive, but she gets to tell him, and he would have been so proud.

We all sit around the bed, holding Mark's hand or touching him. His forehead is hot and Val keeps cool cloths coming to bathe him. Friends started arriving. The tiny room feels cramped. A nurse comes and suggests moving Mark to a bigger room.

By the time they move him more people arrive. The new room is huge, with coffee and tea making facilities and lots of comfortable chairs. I am not aware of time at this point, but friends from all over Auckland start to turn up and not just for a visit; they have come to be with Mark and me and the girls for as long as they can. It doesn't take long for this big room to fill up with people who love us.

Conversations are going in every direction and people seem to be settling in for the long haul. I am sitting on one side of Mark, and David and Val are on the other side. I am overwhelmed at all the people who have come. The space is filled with love, laughter and tears, all at the same time. Mark would love this — and everyone here understands that. Each of them important in Mark's life. The girls and I love the fact that they all want to be here with him, because he is important to them too.

A Little Naughtiness

My attention is diverted by laughing out in the corridor. I get up to investigate and let one of the girls sit closer to Daddy. I search out the source of the commotion and find Neil Carter and Katherine Pether racing each other, one in a stolen wheelchair and the other with a walker commandeered from somewhere. I crack up laughing.

Our friendship has always consisted of Mark and Kath being the loud rebels and Kath's husband Stephen and I being the sensible ones, so of course why would this change when Mark is dying. Mark would love that Kath and Neil were having some fun.

'You know Stephen, if it wasn't Mark dying on that bed, he would be the one who would have stolen the wheelchair and racing Kath and Neil right now.'

Stephen nods; 'Absolutely!'

As the afternoon wears on, I feel the need for fresh air, and I head down the corridor, to a balcony spot overlooking the hospital entrance. As I lean over the railing one of the doctors familiar with Mark's situation spots me and comes over.

'How are you doing?' she asks.

'I'm not sure. Would you be able to explain to me exactly what is happening to Mark, inside his brain?'

She hesitates and then says, 'as the brain is filling up with blood, Mark's body will slowly be shutting down.'

'We noticed Mark's legs and hands are very cold yet his forehead is burning up,' I say.

'Yes, the brain will work hard to make sure vital organs keep working, but it will slowly stop being able to do that, and eventually everything will shut down. His heart will be the last thing to stop.'

'Wow. . . okay then, thank you.'

Somehow knowing in more detail what is occurring makes it a little less scary. I go to find Dave and Val to tell them. As we sit once again in the family room out of earshot of everyone else, Katherine comes running in and announces, 'Mark's breathing has changed, and I think you should come.'

I jump up and run across the corridor into our big family room where Mark is lying and everyone is drawing closer to the bed. His breathing is shallow and slow. I realize everyone in the room knows that this is it; Mark is leaving this earth and about to enter his eternal home.

I grab his hand and draw close to him. 'Mark, I love you, I love you so much, please don't go. Please!' Tears run down my cheeks and all over Mark's face as I kiss him good-bye. The girls are hugging him, too, and one by one saying they love him. All I feel is shock, unbelief and heartache.

I want God's peace to show up, I want a vision of heaven – I want something to ease the awful pain of this moment. But heaven is silent on earth as it prepares to welcome one of its loved ones home. Mark's breathing is slowing down and then I hear nothing. Silence. A nurse listens to his heart with a stethoscope; it makes a couple more attempts at beating and then no more. The time is 4:50 p.m. on the 3rd of December 2009.

CHAPTER
TWENTY-NINE
AND NOW MY LIFESONG SINGS

'For when your eyes are on this child, Your grace abounds to me' - Keith Green – 'Oh Lord You're Beautiful.'

JUST LIKE that someone leaves this earth. Mark's body is lying in front of me, but there is no life. He has gone; he has taken nothing with him, he has left us. Gone. Our bodies truly are a shell without the spirit/ soul. As he lies there motionless, the sobbing starts from around the room. It is the most heart-breaking, unbelievable moment when you know the person you love is never going to be with you again. Never going to talk, laugh, joke, hug or say, 'I love you' again.

My brother Rob comes and wraps his arms around me and lets me sob. I forget about my girls, I cannot focus on anything but the pain I am feeling. My husband is dead, the father of my girls is dead, my best friend is dead. Dead, dead, dead. I can't bear the overwhelmingly intense pain. I hate it. I want it to stop, to go away.

Rob loosens his grip and I look up and see others have surrounded the girls, but all are mourning the loss of this very special husband, father, son, and friend. I feel a panic attack coming. I don't have a clue what I am supposed to do next. Dad tries to calm me down , but I scream at him, 'I don't know what to do now; I don't know what to do with Mark.' I have to do something, but I have absolutely no idea what that something is.

When the funeral directors arrive to take Mark's body away I feel another struggle to release control. 'I want him to come home. You are supposed to bring him back home,' I insist.

The funeral director replies calmly; 'We will take Mark now and get him looking nice. I will come in the morning to get his clothes that you want him to wear and you can pick the casket, then we will bring him home later that day.

I don't want him to go. I don't want him out of my sight. I have been married to him for nearly twenty years and for the last ten years, I have been fully responsible for him, for his care and welfare. I do not want him to go anywhere except to stay with me.

She goes out to the hearse and comes back in with a big dark red velvet blanket. To my shock she covers his face as well as his body with the blanket and with a colleague loads him onto a trolley to take him out to their waiting vehicle.

She closes the door and begins to pull away. I cannot control myself. I scream, 'No, No, no!' Dad comes over to calm me down. I fling my arms around trying to get free and chase the car. I think I hit him, but he lets go when he sees I am not running far. I stand devastated watching the black hearse disappear.

Nothing Prepares For Loss

I find myself sitting in the back of my big van heading away from the hospital. My brother Rob is driving and all the girls are in the van with us. No one is talking. I am looking out the window wondering, did that really happen? Is Mark really dead? Am I really going home without him? Am I really a widow? This is something I thought I was prepared for and the fact is, I am not at all prepared.

We arrive home at about 7: 00 p.m. to lots of people in the house and Rob's wife Katja cooking yummy food. I head for the couch in our dining area. I sit and I cry. The house is buzzing with activity and as more people arrive so does more food. I just sit and cry. Word of Mark's death has spread quickly. Neighbors arrive offering their homes for people to stay in and the phone is busy with incoming and outgoing calls.

I want to tell Steve and Cathy who are still in China. I start asking repeatedly for someone to contact them. Val comes to the rescue and gets on the computer and sends them an e-mail. Dad rings my brother Adam and his wife Raelene in Australia and David rings Mark's brother Phillip in America. I just sit and cry. People find a bed or leave. Sleep eludes me. At 3: 00 a.m. I get up and write a status on Facebook so friends around the world will know. Mark is dead.

Hope And A Future

December 4, 2009: My husband died yesterday – died. Shock has taken over from the tears. I get up to face my day. The funeral director arrives in the morning to sort out the arrangements. We choose the cheapest of an ugly bunch of caskets (what does it really matter, I think) and select the wording for the newspaper death notice. Then she leaves taking the clothes I had prepared for Mark to wear. I can't wait for him to come home, everything feels wrong without him.

My house is a railway station with a constant stream of people, of coffee being made and food being handed around. It is nearly 3: 00 p.m. when the hearse arrives with Mark's body in its casket. He is wheeled into the house, the lid comes off and we all get to see him. It is so surreal; he looks asleep – not dead. I breathe a sigh of relief. It is so good to have him home. I don't feel so overwhelmed or sad. He is where he is supposed to be; he is home.

The days that follow are a whirlwind of people and funeral arrangements. Mark died six days before our twentieth wedding anniversary. I decide that the funeral will be at the same church (First Presbyterian) and same time (1: 00 p.m.) where we said our marriage vows. The casket has an ugly frilly satin fabric lining that Mark would hate, so we have covered it with Mark's blanket and now it really looks like he is just asleep.

Belinda has brought permanent markers so people can write and draw on the casket and the lid. It gives everyone a chance to write their final good-byes. It is so cool reading what everyone has written, especially the kids. Family and friends arrive from overseas; Mark's brother Phillip from the US, and my brother Adam from Australia. Misha and Bonnie's friends stay over, so they are spending most of their time in their rooms with their friends.

I am intrigued with how my mind has reacted these last few days. When Mark first died I had no peace, and no comfort. I started stressing over whether heaven was real, and I was anxious Mark wasn't there at all. As I spilled all my fears out to the Lord, a peace that I can't explain slowly ebbed its way into my home and my mind. The scripture that keeps resonating in my head is Jeremiah 29: 11, '" For I know the plans I have for you," says the Lord. "They are plans for good not for disaster, to give you a future and a hope.'"

I feel very strongly that part of this promise of a future and a hope is our eternal home and that Mark is now there, healed and living in that promise.

We have had some funny moments. Someone brought Mark a can of Dr. Pepper and placed it in the casket. There was much debate about what would happen to it if it was left there for the cremation ceremony. Bonnie decided that it was her duty, on behalf of her father, to solve the problem and drank it.

I spend a lot of time sitting by the casket holding Mark's hand, knowing soon I will never be able to touch him again. As cold as it is, it is still him. It is so healing having his body at home before the final good-bye of the funeral. We have all got to see that the life has truly left him. Over our five days of mourning, it truly sinks in as Psalm 103: 15– 16 says, 'As for man, his days are like grass, he flourishes like a flower of the field; the wind blows over it and it is gone, and its place remembers it no more' (NKJV).

See You In Heaven

December 8, 2009: The day of the funeral has arrived so quickly. Part of me is grateful because the circus that is my home is exhausting, but part of me is nervous – am I really going to my husband's funeral? At the end of today I will never see or touch him again, and very soon everyone will leave and the girls and I will be left to confront the reality that there are now only five of us. I bought waterproof mascara and pencil eyeliner, trying my best to look nice for this sad occasion.

We stand around crying as the guys put the lid over Mark. This is it; never will we see him again. It is an overwhelmingly sad moment. Then Stephen Pether hands out strips of duct tape for us to stick on the casket. Anyone who knows Mark knows his favourite tool was always duct tape, evident by the numerous items like remotes and phones that are still in view fixed with a piece of duct tape. Soon the sides of his coffin are a mess of silver tape – it is perfect!

I want to tell Mark about all this. I want to talk to him about him dying. I want to talk to him about the girls and how they watched him die. I want to tell him about all the many people who love us and have dropped everything to be here for him as he entered eternity, and now were here for me and the girls. I want to tell him I don't want to do this.

I want to tell him I am going to his funeral, and it isn't right. Since I was eighteen years old, Mark is the person I shared everything with, every minute ridiculous detail has fallen on his ears and now he isn't here and that alone is horrible.

There is a big line of cars outside the church. The hymn "Amazing Grace" is playing as the men carry Mark in, followed by his Mum, and then me and the girls carry flowers, which we place on the casket once Mark is settled on the dais.

Jordan Carter has written on the end of Mark's casket in big letters, 'see you in heaven' — now fully displayed to everyone. How perfect, I think to myself, a vivid reminder of the fact that this life is not all there is. Mark is in heaven and one day we are going to be there with him.

Our dear friend Jack Foster, who was pastor of First Presbyterian Church when we came back from missions from1998 to 2003, is officiating. Mark always wanted Jack to do his funeral. Jack and Carole are such special people in our lives and have walked with us during the first few years in a big way. Jack is just what a pastor should be, and he does a beautiful job reminding us of Mark's sense of humor, and the fun times, but also the fact that this is still a very sad day. Most importantly Jack shares, "He was a man of faith. He loved the Lord."

We play two awesome video tributes to Mark. Tibor (Mark's work friend) had done one to the U2 song "Beautiful Day." It was mostly photos of Mark when he was well. The second, to

MISSING YOU

a Casting Crowns track, "Lifesong" is shots of Mark during his illness, many of them involving him clowning around with family and friends. Mark had picked two songs to be played during the service by a band made up of some of his best mates. They are Keith Green's "Oh Lord You're Beautiful" and Hillsong's "Till I See You."

Then his Dad, David, speaks and shares about Jesus and the reality of heaven where Mark now lives. Phillip tells us all how he always looked up to his big brother who seemed larger than life. Adam shares about Mark being a brother , not 'just' a brother 'n law and how cool he always was. And incredibly cute and brave eleven-year-old Emerald tells everyone how Dad always played Barbie with her.

Then it is my turn. I start with reading some e-mails I have received from overseas.

From Richard Colbrook, Oxford, England

Subject: With love from Oxford, England.

Dear Suz,

You may remember our e-mail conversation a year or so ago. I'm a pastor of a church and I contacted you about a family whose son had bone cancer and who had become Christians through watching you and Mark on the Journeys DVDs.

We wanted to drop you a line because Rob Harley contacted us to tell me about Mark. We simply wanted to say that we are very sorry and that we and the church here are praying for you and your girls. We send daily prayer text messages out to about seventy people and one has just been sent out for you.

We did want to say something to you and hope this is a small comfort. Mark will meet people in heaven from Oxford, including Jake Spicer (the lad with bone cancer) who died in July. The people will all tell him a similar story – that they are there because they discovered that Christianity is relationship and not religion and that they discovered this principally through watching Journeys.

Of all of the lives documented in Journeys it is yours and Mark's that are the most impacting and are the key to people wanting to seriously find a relationship with God for themselves. Journeys is increasingly being used all over England and we hear lots of stories of people being saved through it.

We were in the North East of the country last week helping three new church plants – all three will be planted by lost people being saved through Journeys.

We are reminded of something Charles Spurgeon once said:

"He that winneth souls is wise because he has selected a wise object. I think it was Michelangelo who once carved certain magnificent statues in snow. They are gone; the material readily compacted by the frost as readily melted in the heat.

"Far wiser was he when he fashioned the enduring marble and produced works which will last all down the ages. But even marble itself is consumed and fretted by the tooth of time; and he is wise who selects for his raw material immortal souls, whose existence shall outlast the stars.

"If God shall bless us to the winning of souls, our work shall remain when the wood, and hay, and stubble of earth's art and science shall have gone to the dust from which they sprang. In heaven itself, the soul-winner, blessed of God, shall have memorials of his work preserved forever in the galleries of the skies."

From all that we have heard, it is clear that Mark was an amazing man and whatever we say at this time will seem very superficial. However, we did simply want to say that when we all get to heaven there will be hundreds if not thousands of souls there – memorials preserved forever in the galleries of the skies.

These thousands will be there because they saw the faith of you and your husband on a DVD and decided that they wanted a friendship with Jesus Christ like yours.

We will be praying for you and your girls now in an on-going way. Lesley Spicer (Jake's mum) and their family send their love.

Much love, Rich & Kate

And another from Charlotte in England:

Dear Suz, I know you don't know me, but by being part of the world wide church, we felt we got to know a little of you through Mark's story in the Journeys DVD and Life Stories DVD.

I am so sorry to hear of the death of your brave Mark. His composure and desire to love his family in such difficult times brought such light to the many who have watched your story with me. Many have become Jesus followers and make up our church here.

Your candid honesty, determination to keep going and the story of God meeting you in some very difficult times gave us all so much hope. I wish you could meet all the friends who you will meet in heaven because of your broken story. You will be amazed!

I heard from Rob Harley that Mark had died a few hours after I had been watching Life Stories (your episode). It seemed so significant. The ladies who watched it with me are starting out on the journey of following Jesus. When we heard that Mark had died, even that sad news was described by these friends as 'a relief'. He had fought so hard. You have fought a good fight.

I am not really able to imagine what your life must feel like. It must be very sad to at last let go of Mark and to face a future without him when you have been so used to his presence. I pray you will recover steadily, find your equilibrium and know that you are still loved and such a bright star. Although you do not know me, I am sure the angels cheer over the mention of Mark and Suz Holmes' names. We do. Keep going girl – you are one in a zillion.

With very much love, thanks for shining and prayers from England. Charlotte x

I then continued with a reading from Jeremiah 29: 11, 'For I know the plans I have for you, says the Lord, plans for good and not for evil. Plans to give you a future and a hope.'

'In the last six days since Mark's death I have asked God to reveal Himself to me, to show me He still has me in the palm of His hand and to confirm to me that Mark is now reveling in the glories of heaven.

'As I sought God for this He led me to the verse I have just read to you. For I know the plans I have for you and for Mark, He said, plans for good and not for evil, plans to give you a future and a hope.

'As I spent time meditating on this verse, God made it clear to me that this promise is two sided, it is for this side of eternity – the time we spend on this earth in our physical bodies, but even more so, it is for the other side of eternity.

'You see, this future and this hope He promises is heaven. The reality is the last nine and a half years have not been good for Mark. God used it for good with our story being shared around the world through Journeys and Life Stories.

'God used it for good to bring people into a relationship with Jesus. God used it for good in letting the girls know their Dad for six years longer than they could have. But in Mark's everyday life there was not a lot of goodness in the pain, vomiting and constant seizures. God was still there in it, but it wasn't always good.

'But God never saw it just from our limited view; He always saw Mark's life with eternity, and with the wonders of heaven around the corner. God promised Mark a future and a hope and on the 3rd of December 2009 at 4: 50 p.m. Mark entered that promise. For us there is grief now, but there is an element of joy to know Mark is finally home.

'"For I know the plans I have for you, says the Lord, plans for good and not for evil, plans to give you a future and a hope." This is also our promise for those of us left here; our time has not come for us to go to our final hope of our heavenly home.

'We still have things to do, and those things will be for good and not for evil. For God, the Almighty, all powerful, amazing creator of the universe, knows the plans He has for me, for my children, for all of us and they are for good and they are full of hope, but let us never lose sight of the hope and future that will one day be ours too when we enter our eternal home.

'For God knows the plan He had for Mark, for a future and a hope with Him forever. Praise our wonderful redeemer for taking Mark to that hope!'

PART VI–
END GAME

'The will of God will not take us where the grace of God
cannot sustain us.'
Billy Graham.
2011 – 2012

LETTER TO MARK

18 Months Later
May 26, 2011.

Dear Mark,

THERE IS so incredibly much I want to say to you and yet you are not here, and will never be again. How does one wrap their head around that? I can't. I want to turn around and see you there, well again. I want to wake up from this very bad long nightmare and find it is over.

Nothing prepares you for death. I so many times thought I was ready – HA! What did I know? I was ready for nothing! I was a fool! Such a bloody fool!

The first thing I want to tell you is you died, you actually died. You were breathing and then your breathing slowed down and then stopped and a few minutes later your heart stopped too. The moment was so unreal. I want to talk to you about it; I want you to tell me what you were feeling, what you heard? Was Jesus there waiting? Was He saying it was time? Was He comforting you? Did you feel joy and peace? But I can't ask you because you are gone. I was left and the person I was supposed to grow old with died. I often want to scream at you, HOW

COULD YOU LEAVE ME? How could you do that? I thought you loved me. Still, eighteen months down the track I ask, how could you leave me?

How could you leave me to raise these four daughters of ours on my own? I can't do it Mark and I'm not doing it well. They are such hard work all of the time. I know they are going through their own grief too, but parenting them is a hopeless cause. I suck at it. Mark, I want to stop the world and get off. I want to run into a cave and scream, 'Leave me alone.' I just want to go away, go away and grieve. Not have to do anything else but that. I miss you so much. You had no idea about the pain of losing someone for good. It hurts so much.

I miss our marriage, the hope, the future, the sharing. I feel alone all the time. No one is really on my side. The girls aren't, most of the time I don't think they care about me; it's just what I can do for them or give them that they care about.

Everyone has their opinion on all areas of my life, but no one is sharing my life to really care, only me, just me. I am on my own. You, you who were supposed to be there till I got old, you left. I want to hit you so hard sometimes because I am so mad at you for going. Now there you are in eternity, surrounded by God's incredible love, and in complete joy. Here I am left on earth where it all sucks.

It's all so hard on my own. Everything feels so incredibly heavy. Finances are a constant worry. The girls and their behavior is a constant stress. Working is horrible, especially on Saturdays. All the household chores seem huge. It's all too big and hard.

My birthday is coming up. I know no-one will really make an effort. Well my friends might, but my children won't. It is five days after the ball so all their money will go to that. You cared;

you made an effort. Mark, I miss someone making an effort, who cared for me, who really loved me.

Misha has a serious boyfriend. I see he is becoming significant to her and it is very hard to accept I am no longer that important in her life. I wish you were here to meet him, to do the Dad thing and be scary. I have to play good cop, bad cop, and believe me, it doesn't work so well.

Mark, if I could wish for anything it would be to talk over all the issues that I'm facing with the girls with you, with the other person who loved them as much as me, to sit for a couple of hours and just go over all the details. How I miss that part of our partnership.

Mark, I also want to say sorry, sorry for the years I didn't cope with your illness. Sorry I wasn't compassionate and caring. When you got sick I lost so much. Our marriage was so good; you were an amazing husband and father. I just never really coped with all that I lost, with all that was stolen from me by cancer and necrosis. I wish that I was better at looking after you; I'm so sorry.

And I'm so sorry for the last day. You were conscious for half an hour on that Thursday. I had no idea how serious the situation was. In truth, half of me thought you were being a drama queen about the pain – guess you weren't. I wish so much I had known, or had even stopped to assess the situation. That last half hour haunted me so much I sought counselling for it within the first year. I kept beating myself up – why did I always just focus on the task? The counselling helped me forgive myself. I needed to move past the guilt. But there is no excuse for my behavior; sometimes I'm a bitch. I only really freaked out when you went unconscious; up until that point I thought I had things pretty much under control although I couldn't get you dressed. Nothing ever prepared me for not coming home with you that day.

It was so bloody awful when your body was taken away by the funeral director. They moved you from the bed you had been in onto a wheelie bed and then she covered your entire body with that velvet cloth, including your face.

It felt so final, so over. I wanted to scream that there had been some massive mistake, but I didn't. I just followed your body to the hearse and watched them push you in. It was so awful, so very awful.

I wonder what you were doing then? Were you being welcomed into heaven by many people? Did you see your grandparents or mine? Did you meet your brother or sister that your Mum miscarried? What was it like? So many questions never to be answered.

I read today that nothing can ever separate us from God's love, death can't and life can't. That means both you and I are still surrounded by it. I don't feel it much lately, most of the time I just feel alone, overwhelmed and tired. But regardless, the word of God is true, so that means I am not separated from God's love. You however are basking in it; slightly unfair don't you think?

I wish I could ask you to pray for me but I cannot talk to you. Mark, I want to make the most of what life I do have left. I want to use every breath to tell people about Jesus and what he's done. I'm not doing that, I suck! Put on this earth to do a job and I am not doing it. I so want to, but I feel like there is this blockade in my way. I wish you were here, supporting me, helping me, standing beside me. I wish I wasn't alone.

I love you Mark. I always did and I always will. Thank you for the first ten years of our marriage. Thank you for loving me, for my four daughters, little living pieces of you. Thank you for treating me so well. And then thank you for somehow still loving me through those awful years of your illness. Thank you for still listening to me and for putting up with my behavior. Thank you.

One day I am going to go where you are. One day Jesus is going to lead me to my eternal home and one day I am going to see you again. I hope between now and then I make you and Jesus proud of me. I hope on the day when Jesus leads me to eternity, you are the first person there to welcome me home.

Until that day. . . Love Suz

FINAL WORD

'It is not the strength of the body, but the strength of the spirit.' – J.R.R. Tolkien.

Three Years Later.
November 26, 2012.

IN A WEEK it will be three years since Mark died. One thousand ninety-five days to be exact. What has changed? What have I learned? Who have I become? With something so incredibly huge happening in a person's life, it cannot help but define them, change them. It becomes a part of us for better or for worse.

Three years ago I wondered if I would ever recover, three years ago I wondered if I would ever hope again. Sometimes it hurt just to breathe; sometimes I would wake up in the morning and wish I was waking up from an incredibly bad dream. Within seconds I would remember the reality. So three years. . .

Well first I have come to realize I will always have a sadness in my life. I loved Mark; during his illness I often felt like I hated him, but in actual fact I always loved him and he is gone. I will always miss him, how could I not? People don't become less important in your life because they are not here – they are just not here.

But this sadness doesn't feel like a bad thing anymore. It reminds me I was once so loved; it reminds me I have loved deeply, and it reminds me of Mark. None of that can be viewed as bad, because it is not. This sadness is part of me and is in a really weird way a comfort – I guess that comfort is the knowledge of the past and that is something I never want to lose.

Secondly three years down the track I feel whole. Suffering makes us whole. We have to walk through it, in all its many and varied forms, but to be a whole person, to be complete I have come to believe we must endure suffering.

Feeling whole is so nice, as I face the world and as I talk to people about my journey, I can talk from this steady place. I have been through the darkest of moments, and now here I stand. I survived, and not only did I survive I have grown, and not only have I grown I have become whole. I like this.

The girls: my greatest treasure and my greatest source of frustration at times. As I write this I am now the mother of one nineteen-year-old, one eighteen-year-old, one fifteen-year-old and one fourteen-year-old. They are now all my height if not taller, and I honestly cannot believe I am their mother.

There is no way I am old enough, but apparently I am. I look at them and it gives me the greatest pleasure to see a little of Mark in each. I think I see it more because he is not here, and it is so obvious when they do things like him. Emerald's hair is exactly like Mark's before he got dreads. I love looking at it. It reminds me of the early fun days in our marriage. I love that she has this blatant piece of Mark. But they all look a little like him. So often people remark 'the girls look so like you,' and I think 'if only you had met their Dad.'

Solo parenting sucks big time. I salute every solo parent out there and say, 'You are my hero!' I am tired all the time, and for Pete's sake they aren't even toddlers. Here's a piece of advice: Teenagers are just as time consuming and exhausting as toddlers and babies – it's just different. To be honest I hate parenting on my own, I didn't have four children to do this on my own and this is probably one of the biggest things I shake my fist at God about still.

However, somehow He does give me the strength each day and although I am honest enough to say I probably very rarely get this parenting thing right, I am trying my best and do feel a bit wiser than I did three years ago.

I am sure God will continue to hear this complaint for many years to come, as parenting is never the same from one day to the next and each of my girls is different – not to mention those delightful things called hormones. I am convinced that when my youngest one turns twenty-one I should be made a Dame for surviving four teenage daughters. Believe me it is no small task.

As to the working situation, well my girls have started calling me 'a job whore.' Not the most complimentary title, but unfortunately I do have to own it. I am just finishing my third job this year and about to start my fourth, but have been offered five in total. The first job wasn't enough hours, the second job wasn't enough pay, I got offered a job between number two and number three and that was both not enough hours or pay, number three job hasn't worked out because of too many nights and weekends, so hence job number four is commencing next Tuesday.

To be honest, I feel like this is an area where I have really floundered – kind of obvious! I did not expect to be working and being the sole provider for my family. I still can't really wrap my head around that I am and actually I suck at this too.

Having absolutely no qualifications apart from one year at Bible College really has paid a huge part in not being able to get a really good paying job. Because I didn't go to University or get a trade – I am pretty worthless money wise.

But I look back and there is not a part of my past I would not do again, so I do have to trust that God who has led me this far will continue. Hopefully one day I will be able to do what I really want to. What is that I hear you ask? (Well not really, but just in case you did ask.)

I just want to spend every day encouraging people to give God a go. Without Him I would have failed big time. I know that I have failed, but I would have done a much worse job without Him. This book is a little of that desire.

As you can well imagine my priorities are very different. Things aren't important, people are. I try each day to remember that and let it dictate my actions and decisions. All of Mark's precious guitar gear is now stored in the garage. He couldn't take it with him when he left this world, and I will take nothing with me.

It is a very good thing to know and remember. Mark is not remembered and loved because he owned things, but because he loved us and others. His friends don't miss him because he owned cool guitar gear, they miss him because he was their friend and he loved them.

This is a good thing to keep in mind as we live each day. Am I going to be remembered because my house was tidy or I owned a nice car – I hope not! I hope I am remembered because I took the time for people, because they knew I loved them and thought they were important. That, my friends must be our focus – nothing else matters.

My relationship with God has grown too, but in an interesting way. I am a lot more chilled about it. I realise God actually loves me because I'm me and because He loves us all. I know it doesn't matter what I do, His love is not conditional on that.

I do want to please Him and I do want to do what is right and honors Him, but I know He just loves me anyway and will continue to be my strength throughout each day. I wish I could explain this better to those of you who have yet to experience this.

It is like having the strongest help you can possibly imagine beside you and whenever you need to, you can just lean in and it holds you up, supports you and gives out this incredible warmth that you can only compare to love. When I don't have to lean, it is still there, right beside me and I know it without doubt. This is how having a relationship with the God of the universe feels.

As to marriage, amazingly I view it positively. When we say our vows, we say through sickness and through health. The ten years of horribleness with Mark's illness do not overshadow the previous ten years which were full of love, laughter and goodness.

When I think of my marriage to Mark my thoughts instantly remember the good times first, and that is a wonderful gift. Marriage was good. Marriage was hard. But marriage is something I definitely want to do again.

My girls tell me I have to go looking, make an effort. I know in my heart I don't. The Lord brought Mark along and He will bring my next husband along when it is right and both he and I will be in the right place at the right time. I know this without doubt and look forward to seeing this happen.

So that's pretty much it. Three years and things aren't looking too bad. If I had a magic wand I would change it all, none of the illness would have happened, Mark would be alive and be the cool parent I know he would have been.

But I don't have a magic wand and so I live in the reality I have been handed. It is nice to look and think 'It's not too bad' – but there are definitely issues. My finances for one. I don't quite earn enough to make ends meet. That is stressful. Dealing with four daughters and their issues is another. Teenagers are a struggle. To add to that all my closest family and friends have now left Papakura, and so I am somewhat alone. However, I know from experience it will be good again.

I am content, I am excited, I am apprehensive, I am nervous, I love, I am loved, I laugh, I cry, I get frustrated, I get angry – I guess this all adds up to I AM ALIVE! Three years down the track I know I am still alive and I still have a responsibility to live and make the most of the life I have been given.

Mark's illness and death took the wind out of my sails for a long time. I felt myself drag through the days. Now his illness and death gives me something I didn't expect. It gives me a voice of experience, it's given me an amazing relationship with Jesus and it has given me wholeness. It gives me a springboard to live from – and this truly is surprising.

THE END

THE GOOD NEWS

I want to tell you about my favourite thing. The Gospel of Jesus Christ!

In the Bible it is also called the Good News, and it is good, in fact it's the great news!!!

(Romans 1:1-4, Romans 1:16-17, 1 Thessalonians 1:5, 1 Corinthians 15:1-8)

Why is it my favourite? Well…

Jesus came!

The God of the universe came to earth in the form of the man we know as Jesus.

(John 1:1-3, John 1:10, John 1:14, John 1:18, John 3:4-8, Genesis 1: 1-2, Genesis 1:26 Philippians 2:6)

Jesus lived a human life.

He showed us how to live life with love and compassion. In the New Testament books in the Bible, Matthew, Mark, Luke & John we can read about his miracles, his teachings, and how he interacted with others. It is a wonderful challenge that shows us how to live a life like Jesus; a life of putting God first in all things, and loving and serving others.

(Mark 12: 30-31, Matthew 22:37-40, Luke 10:27, Matthew 23:11-12)

Jesus died.

He was executed on a cross even though he had never done anything wrong. Jesus' sacrifice took everything we have ever done wrong and cleanses us if we just believe. That sacrifice was needed so you and I could have a personal relationship with the Most Holy God.

(Matthew 27:32-66, Mark 15:21-47, Luke: 26-56, John 19:16-42, Romans 3:21-31, Romans 5:8, 1 John 4:10, Isaiah 53, Titus 2:14)

Jesus rose from the dead!

He defeated death and gave us the hope and home of eternity with him. Heaven is real and Jesus is preparing a place for us there once our time here is over. All we have to do is believe in Jesus and our eternity is secured with him – this is so awesome!

(Matthew 28:1-10, Mark 16:1-8, Luke 24:1-12, John 20, Acts 2:30-32, Acts 4:32-34, 1 Corinthians 15:55-57, John 14:1-4)

Lastly Jesus sent his Holy Spirit!

God here but this time never leaving and actually able to fill us. The Holy Spirit teaches us, helps us understand the Bible, and works through us so we can be obedient to the teachings of Jesus.

(John 14:26, Matthew 3:11, Matthew 28:18-20, Luke 24:49, John 14:17, John 14:26, Acts 1:5, Acts1:8, Acts 2:1-4)

All you have to do is believe! Believe in Jesus and what he did for YOU!!!

Here is a prayer if you would like to accept what Jesus did for you:

Jesus, I believe you came, you died and you rose for me.

I ask you to forgive all the things I have done wrong and come into my life.

I give my life to you, believing you are Lord of all and now Lord of my life.

Amen!

The next steps are easy:

1. Get yourself a Bible, there are lots of different versions so find one that is easy for you to read and understand. Read it!!!

2. Pray – this is just chatting to God. He loves us to chat and tell him everything and ask him to help with it all.

3. Find a church – so important to be around others who love Jesus and will help you in your new relationship with him!

If you want you can send me an email telling me of your decision and I would love to pray for you and answer any questions! This is the best decision you will ever make!!!!

(The Scriptures on this page are by no means exhaustive)

NOTE FROM SUZ

Thank you for reading Missing You, Finding Hope in Hardship. My prayer is that through reading this book you have come to know Jesus a little better and despite what life throws at you He will be the one you seek refuge, strength and help from.

If you did find this book helpful and enjoyed it please help other readers find this book:

1. This book is lendable, so send it to a friend who you think might like it.
2. I welcome the opportunity to speak to groups about faith in tough times. Please contact me if you feel you would like me to share.
3. Please feel free to contact me at **iamsuzholmes@gmail. com**. I would love to pray for you so please don't hesitate to let me know what is going on in your life.
4. Come like my **Facebook** page I am Suz Holmes or read my blog **suzholmes.com**